Romantics to the Present Day
An Anthology of Poetry

Edited by Seamus Perry and David Womersley

UNIVERSITY PRESS

UNIVERSITY PRESS

Great Clarendon Street, Oxford, OX2 6DP, United Kingdom

Oxford University Press is a department of the University of Oxford.
It furthers the University's objective of excellence in research, scholarship,
and education by publishing worldwide. Oxford is a registered trade mark of
Oxford University Press in the UK and in certain other countries

© Oxford University Press 2017

The moral rights of the authors have been asserted

All rights reserved. No part of this publication may be reproduced, stored in a
retrieval system, or transmitted, in any form or by any means, without the prior
permission in writing of Oxford University Press, or as expressly permitted
by law, by licence or under terms agreed with the appropriate reprographics
rights organization. Enquiries concerning reproduction outside the scope of the
above should be sent to the Rights Department, Oxford University Press, at the
address above.

You must not circulate this work in any other form
and you must impose this same condition on any acquirer

British Library Cataloguing in Publication Data

Data available

ISBN 978-019-839627-7

1 3 5 7 9 10 8 6 4 2

Printed in China by Golden Cup

Contents

Introduction	5
Youth, Age, and Death: Growing Up, Growing Old	7
Anna Laeticia Barbauld (1743–1825) *To a Little Invisible Being who is Expected Soon to Become Visible*	8
Anne Stevenson (b. 1933) *Poem for a Daughter*	10
Carol Ann Duffy (b. 1955) *A Child's Sleep*	11
Samuel Taylor Coleridge (1772–1834) From *Frost at Midnight*	12
Jon Silkin (1930–1997) *Death of a Son (who died in a mental hospital aged one)*	14
Hugo Williams (b. 1942) *Mirrors, Windows*	16
Ted Hughes (1930–1998) *Full Moon and Little Frieda*	17
William Wordsworth (1770–1850) From *The Two-Part Prelude, Book I*	18
Charles Causley (1917–2003) *Timothy Winters*	20
Stephen Spender (1909–1995) *My Parents*	22
Arundhathi Subramaniam (b. 1973) *I Speak for Those with Orange Lunch Boxes*	23
E.J. Scovell (1907–1999) *Growing Girl*	24
Leontia Flynn (b. 1974) *My Father's Language*	25
D.H. Lawrence (1885–1930) *Piano*	26
Thomas Hardy (1840–1928) *The Self-Unseeing*	27
Emily Jane Brontë (1818–1848) *Remembrance*	28
Christina Rossetti (1830–1894) *Remember*; *Song*	30
A.E. Housman (1859–1936) *To an Athlete Dying Young*	32
Edmund Blunden (1896–1974) *Forefathers*	34
Mary Webb (1881–1927) *Going for the Milk*	36
James Henry (1798–1876) *Another and Another and Another*	37
e.e. cummings (1894–1962) *anyone lived in a pretty how town*	38
Alfred Tennyson (1809–1892) *Crossing the Bar*	40

Love, Family, and Relationships: The Bonds Between Us   41
Robert Burns (1759–1796) *The Rigs o' Barley*   42
George Gordon, Lord Byron (1788–1824)   From *Don Juan*   44
Elizabeth Barrett Browning (1806–1861)   From *Sonnets from the Portuguese*   47
Robert Browning (1812–1889) *Meeting at Night*   48
Alfred Tennyson (1809–1892) *The Miller's Daughter*   49
William Morris (1834–1896) *Love is Enough*   50
Robert Bridges (1844–1930) *Awake, my Heart, to be loved*   51
Robert Frost (1875–1963) *Putting in the Seed*   52
James Fenton (b. 1949) *Hinterhof*   53
Seamus Heaney (1939–2013) *Digging*   54
Grace Nichols (b. 1950) *Praise Song for My Mother*   56
Tony Harrison (b. 1937) *Clearing I*   57
Norman MacCaig (1910–1996) *Aunt Julia*   58
Kate Tempest (b. 1985) *For my Niece*   60
Simon Armitage (b. 1963) *Poem*   61
Percy Bysshe Shelley (1792–1822) *When the Lamp is Shattered*   62
William Blake (1757–1827) *Love's Secret*   64
John Keats (1795–1821) *In Drear-Nighted December*   65
Charlotte Mew (1869–1928) *À Quoi Bon Dire*   66
A.E. Housman (1859–1936) *The rain, it streams on stone and hillock*   67
Robert Burns (1759–1796) *Auld Lang Syne*   68
Tracey Herd (b. 1968) *You Can't Take My World from Me*   70

Wild Things and Natural Places: The World Around Us   71
John Clare (1793–1864) *Open Winter*   72
Philip Larkin (1922–1985) *The Trees*   73
Edna St. Vincent Millay (1892–1950) *The Death of Autumn*   74
Philip Larkin (1922–1985) *First Sight*   75
Thomas Hardy (1840–1928) *The Darkling Thrush*   76
Bernard O'Donoghue (b. 1945) *The Robin in Autumn*   78
Jo Shapcott (b. 1953) *Cabbage Dreams*   79
D.H. Lawrence (1885–1930) *Snake*   80
Emily Dickinson (1830–1886) *The Snake*   84
Elizabeth Bishop (1911–1979) *The Fish*   85
Robert Burns (1759–1796) *To A Mouse*   88

William Blake (1757–1827) *The Lamb*; *The Tyger*	90
Kathleen Jamie (b. 1962) *White-Sided Dolphins*	92
Ted Hughes (1930–1998) *The Jaguar*	93
Alfred Tennyson (1809–1892) *The Eagle*; *The Kraken*	94
'Lewis Carroll' [Charles Lutwidge Dodgson] (1832–1898) *Jabberwocky*	96
Sophie Hannah (b. 1971) *Squirrel's the Word*	98
Roger McGough (b. 1937) *Bad Day at the Ark*	99
Gerard M. Hopkins (1844–1899) *Pied Beauty*	100
Power, Conflict, and Violence: Inflicted Harms	101
Robert Southey (1774–1843) *After Blenheim*	102
Rupert Brooke (1887–1915) *The Soldier*	105
Charles Wolfe (1791–1823) *The Burial of Sir John Moore after Corunna*	106
Robert Browning (1812–1889) *Incident of the French Camp*	108
Arthur Hugh Clough (1819–1861) From *Amours de Voyage*	110
Henry Newbolt (1862–1938) *He fell among Thieves*	113
W.B. Yeats (1865–1939) *An Irish Airman Foresees His Death*	116
Siegfried Sassoon (1886–1967) *The General*	117
Isaac Rosenberg (1890–1918) *Break of Day in the Trenches*	118
Eva Dobell (1876–1963) *In a Soldiers' Hospital I: Pluck*	119
Wilfred Owen (1893–1918) *Disabled*	120
Vernon Scannell (1922–2007) *Walking Wounded*	122
Mary Postgate Cole (1893–1980) *The Veteran*	124
Michael Symmons Roberts (b. 1963) *The Order*	125
Choman Hardi (b. 1974) *Gas Attack*	126
Roger McGough (b. 1937) *The End of Summer*	127
Imitiaz Dharker (b. 1954) *The right word*	128
Kate Clanchy (b. 1965) *War Poetry*	130
John Keats (1795–1821) From *To J.H. Reynolds, Esq.*	131
John Clare (1793–1864) *Badger*	132
Gerard M. Hopkins (1844–1889) *Binsey Poplars*	134

INTRODUCTION

What is poetry?

There have been many definitions of poetry and, as your familiarity with poetry extends and deepens, you will no doubt come across them. Some will strike a chord with you. Others will move you to impassioned, even furious, dissent.

But, to begin with, think of poetry as memorable speech.

Because poetry is speech, you should be able to hear in all poems a particular voice. A voice which approaches the subject of the poem from a distinctive, sometimes strange or even bewildering, point of view. Unusual words, unusual images, unusual syntax: all these features of poetry are (or should be) dictated by the poet's distinctive point of view.

The distortions of normal speech we encounter in poetry – distortions sometimes mild, sometimes arresting, sometimes outrageous, possibly even offensive – are part of what makes it memorable. And a single poem may include all these different kinds of distortion.

But a poem is also memorable because of the effects of metre and rhyme. Poetry is not only memorable speech. It is also shaped speech. Poetry is shaped not only because (to quote a notorious and apparently flippant, but actually profound, definition of poetry) 'poetry is writing which doesn't reach to the edge of the page'. Poetry is also shaped by the arrangement of emphases within each line to link the lines together and to encourage us to think about how they perhaps pull apart.

You are beginning to explore a form of writing in which, from the very beginning of human society, women and men have tried to capture what for them were the most important parts of their experience.

What could be more challenging?

But also, what could be more exciting?

Seamus Perry
David Womersley

Youth, Age, and Death: Growing Up, Growing Old

To a Little Invisible Being who is Expected Soon to Become Visible

Anna Laetitia Barbauld (1743–1825)

Germ of new life, whose powers expanding slow
For many a moon their full perfection wait—
Haste, precious pledge of happy love, to go
Auspicious borne through life's mysterious gate.

5 What powers lie folded in thy curious frame—
Senses from objects locked, and mind from thought!
How little canst thou guess thy lofty claim
To grasp at all the worlds the Almighty wrought!

And see, the genial season's warmth to share,
10 Fresh younglings shoot, and opening roses glow!
Swarms of new life exulting fill the air—
Haste, infant bud of being, haste to blow[1]!

For thee the nurse prepares her lulling songs,
The eager matrons count the lingering day;
15 But far the most thy anxious parent longs
On thy soft cheek a mother's kiss to lay.

She only asks to lay her burden down,
That her glad arms that burden may resume;
And nature's sharpest pangs her wishes crown,
20 That free thee living from thy living tomb.

She longs to fold to her maternal breast
Part of herself, yet to herself unknown;
To see and to salute the stranger guest,
Fed with her life through many a tedious moon.

25   Come, reap thy rich inheritance of love!
     Bask in the fondness of a Mother's eye!
     Nor wit nor eloquence her heart shall move
     Like the first accents of thy feeble cry.

     Haste, little captive, burst thy prison doors!
30   Launch on the living world, and spring to light!
     Nature for thee displays her various stores,
     Opens her thousand inlets of delight.

     If charmèd verse or muttered prayers had power
     With favouring spells to speed thee on thy way,
35   Anxious I'd bid my beads[2] each passing hour,
     Till thy wished smile thy mother's pangs o'erpay.

                        (c.1795; published 1825)

---

1 blow bloom
2 bid my beads pray using a rosary

Poem for a Daughter

Anne Stevenson (b. 1933)

'I think I'm going to have it,'
I said, joking between pains.
The midwife rolled competent
sleeves over corpulent milky arms.
5 'Dear, you never have it,
we deliver it.'
A judgement years proved true.
Certainly I've never had you

as you still have me, Caroline.
10 Why does a mother need a daughter?
Heart's needle, hostage to fortune,
freedom's end. Yet nothing's more perfect
than that bleating, razor-shaped cry
that delivers a mother to her baby.
15 The bloodcord snaps that held
their sphere together. The child,
tiny and alone, creates the mother.

A woman's life is her own
until it is taken away
20 by a first particular cry.
Then she is not alone
but part of the premises
of everything there is:
a time, a tribe, a war.
25 When we belong to the world
we become what we are.

(1982)

YOUTH, AGE, AND DEATH: GROWING UP, GROWING OLD

A Child's Sleep

Carol Ann Duffy (b. 1955)

I stood at the edge of my child's sleep
hearing her breathe;
although I could not enter there,
I could not leave.

5   Her sleep was a small wood,
perfumed with flowers;
dark, peaceful, sacred,
acred in hours.

And she was the spirit that lives
10 in the heart of such woods;
without time, without history,
wordlessly good.

I spoke her name, a pebble dropped
in the still night,
15 and saw her stir, both open palms
cupping their soft light;

then went to the window. The greater dark
outside the room
gazed back, maternal, wise,
20 with its face of moon.

(1979)

ROMANTICS TO THE PRESENT DAY

From **Frost at Midnight**
Samuel Taylor Coleridge (1772–1834)

> This excerpt is lines 44–74 of a longer work in which the poet, seated alone at night in his rural cottage, and accompanied only by his sleeping infant son, remembers his own isolated childhood at a city school, and contrasts it with the very different future he hopes for his child.

    Dear Babe, that sleepest cradled by my side,
Whose gentle breathings, heard in this deep calm,
Fill up the interspersèd vacancies
And momentary pauses of the thought!
5 My babe so beautiful! it thrills my heart
With tender gladness, thus to look at thee,
And think that thou shalt learn far other lore,
And in far other scenes! For I was reared
In the great city, pent 'mid cloisters dim,
10 And saw nought lovely but the sky and stars.
But *thou*, my babe! shalt wander like a breeze
By lakes and sandy shores, beneath the crags
Of ancient mountain, and beneath the clouds,
Which image in their bulk both lakes and shores
15 And mountain crags: so shalt thou see and hear
The lovely shapes and sounds intelligible
Of that eternal language, which thy God
Utters, who from eternity doth teach
Himself in all, and all things in himself.
20 Great universal Teacher! he shall mould
Thy spirit, and by giving make it ask.

    Therefore all seasons shall be sweet to thee,
Whether the summer clothe the general earth
With greenness, or the redbreast sit and sing

25   Betwixt the tufts of snow on the bare branch
     Of mossy apple-tree, while the nigh thatch
     Smokes in the sun-thaw; whether the eave-drops fall
     Heard only in the trances of the blast,
     Or if the secret ministry[1] of frost
30   Shall hang them up in silent icicles,
     Quietly shining to the quiet Moon.

                                                     (1798)

---

1 ministry the spiritual work or service of a priest

Death of a Son (who died in a mental hospital aged one)

Jon Silkin (1930–1997)

    Something has ceased to come along with me.
Something like a person: something very like one.
        And there was no nobility in it
          Or anything like that.

5   Something was there like a one year
Old house, dumb as stone. While the near buildings
        Sang like birds and laughed
          Understanding the pact

    They were to have with silence. But he
10 Neither sang nor laughed. He did not bless silence
        Like bread, with words.
          He did not forsake silence.

    But rather, like a house in mourning
Kept the eye turned in to watch the silence while
15   The other houses like birds
          Sang around him.

And the breathing silence neither
Moved nor was still.

    I have seen stones: I have seen brick
20 But this house was made up of neither bricks nor stone
        But a house of flesh and blood
          With flesh of stone

     And bricks for blood. A house
   Of stones and blood in breathing silence with the other
       Birds singing crazy on its chimneys.
      But this was silence,

    This was something else, this was
  Hearing and speaking though he was a house drawn
      Into silence, this was
        Something religious in his silence,

    Something shining in his quiet,
  This was different this was altogether something else:
      Though he never spoke, this
        Was something to do with death.

    And then slowly the eye stopped looking
Inward. The silence rose and became still.
The look turned to the outer place and stopped,
     With the birds still shrilling around him.
     And as if he could speak

He turned over on his side with his one year
Red as a wound
He turned over as if he could be sorry for this
And out of his eyes two great tears rolled, like stones,
  and he died.

           (1954)

Mirrors, Windows
Hugo Williams (b. 1942)

You've discovered mirrors are not like windows
And both are dangerous holes in the walls.

You have to go to them, arms jazzing like a flapper[1],
And knock your head where a window suddenly blurs over,

5   Or a mirror wilfully bars entrance on itself.
Not knowing which world one cries into, you look at me

And hit the barrier between us, careful
As it reaches out your hand and touches you.

You seem upset by my two appearances, one tangible,
10 One seen, to your one imprisoned in the screen,

As if that cancelled you. Then turning, you abandon
What you nearly discovered and stagger off, abstracted,

Freed, to an open window where you shout something
At a large dog walking past in the rain.

(1970)

---

1 flapper a lively young woman, fond of dancing and parties

Full Moon and Little Frieda

Ted Hughes (1930–1998)

A cool small evening shrunk to a dog bark and the clank
   of a bucket—
And you listening.
A spider's web, tense for the dew's touch.
5 A pail lifted, still and brimming—mirror
To tempt a first star to a tremor.

Cows are going home in the lane there, looping the hedges
   with their warm wreaths of breath—
A dark river of blood, many boulders,
10 Balancing unspilled milk.

'Moon!' you cry suddenly, 'Moon! Moon!'

The moon has stepped back like an artist gazing
   amazed at a work
That points at him amazed.

(1967)

From **The Two-Part Prelude, Book I**
William Wordsworth (1770–1850)

> This excerpt comes from lines 296–327 of Wordsworth's long autobiography in verse, on which he worked for many years, and which was published under the title *The Prelude* only after his death. In this section he is remembering some of the formative episodes of his early life, which was spent in England's Lake District.

                   I remember well
('Tis of an early season that I speak,
The twilight of rememberable life),
While I was yet an urchin, one who scarce
5 Could hold a bridle, with ambitious hopes
I mounted, and we rode towards the hills.
We were a pair of horsemen: honest James
Was with me, my encourager and guide.
We had not travelled long ere some mischance
10 Disjoined me from my comrade, and, through fear
Dismounting, down the rough and stony moor
I led my horse, and stumbling on, at length
Came to a bottom[1] where in former times
A man, the murderer of his wife, was hung
15 In irons. Mouldered was the gibbet-mast[2];
The bones were gone, the iron and the wood;
Only a long green ridge of turf remained
Whose shape was like a grave. I left the spot,
And reascending the bare slope I saw
20 A naked pool that lay beneath the hills,
The beacon on the summit, and more near
A girl who bore a pitcher on her head
And seemed with difficult steps to force her way
Against the blowing wind. It was in truth

25 An ordinary sight, but I should need
Colours and words that are unknown to man
To paint the visionary dreariness
Which, while I looked all round for my lost guide,
Did at that time invest the naked pool,
30 The beacon on the lonely eminence,
The woman and her garments vexed and tossed
By the strong wind.

(1798; published 1850)

---

1 **bottom** the deepest part of a valley
2 **gibbet-mast** an upright post with projecting arm from which the bodies of criminals were hung in chains or irons after execution

Timothy Winters

Charles Causley (1917–2003)

Timothy Winters comes to school
With eyes as wide as a football pool,
Ears like bombs and teeth like splinters:
A blitz[1] of a boy is Timothy Winters.

5 His belly is white, his neck is dark,
And his hair is an exclamation mark.
His clothes are enough to scare a crow
And through his britches the blue winds blow.

When teacher talks he won't hear a word
10 And he shoots down dead the arithmetic-bird,
He licks the patterns off his plate
And he's not even heard of the Welfare State.

Timothy Winters has bloody feet
And he lives in a house on Suez Street,
15 He sleeps in a sack on the kitchen floor
And they say there aren't boys like him any more.

Old Man Winters likes his beer
And his missus ran off with a bombardier[2],
Grandma sits in the grate with a gin
20 And Timothy's dosed with an aspirin.

The Welfare Worker lies awake
But the law's as tricky as a ten-foot snake,
So Timothy Winters drinks his cup
And slowly goes on growing up.

YOUTH, AGE, AND DEATH: GROWING UP, GROWING OLD

25 At Morning Prayers the Master helves[3]
For children less fortunate than ourselves,
And the loudest response in the room is when
Timothy Winters roars 'Amen!'

So come one angel, come on ten:
30 Timothy Winters says 'Amen
Amen amen amen amen.'
Timothy Winters, Lord.
                Amen.

(1970)

---

1 **blitz** a devastating military attack, designed to create maximum damage; named after the German air attacks on London in 1940

2 **bombardier** a soldier, an artilleryman

3 **helves** Causley, himself a Cornishman, glossed this unusual word as 'a dialect word from north Cornwall used to describe the alarmed lowing of cattle (as when a cow is separated from her calf); a desperate, pleading note'

My Parents

Stephen Spender (1909–1995)

My parents kept me from children who were rough
Who threw words like stones and wore torn clothes.
Their thighs showed through rags. They ran in the street
And climbed cliffs and stripped by the country streams.

5   I feared more than tigers their muscles like iron
Their jerking hands and their knees tight on my arms.
I feared the salt coarse pointing of those boys
Who copied my lisp behind me on the road.

They were lithe, they sprang out behind hedges
10 Like dogs to bark at my world. They threw mud
While I looked the other way, pretending to smile.
I longed to forgive them, but they never smiled.

(1933)

I Speak for Those with Orange Lunch Boxes

Arundhathi Subramaniam (b. 1973)

I speak for those
with orange lunch boxes,

who play third tree
in an orchard of eight
in the annual school play,

who aren't headgirls,
games captains, class monitors,

who watch other girls fight for the seesaw
from the far wall across the sand-pit,

who remember everyone's lines
but their own,

who pelt after the school bus
their mother's breakfasts still heaving
in their gut,

who still believe
there'll be exams one day
they'll be ready for,

Those with orange lunch boxes.
I speak for them.

(2014)

Growing Girl

E.J. Scovell (1907–1999)

Watching from the high brick wall
The younger children's tennis in the lane
Her eyes run thoughtless with the ball,
And the coasts of her face rise clear and plain.

5 Undiscovered or forsaken wholly
Against the sky those slopes and dunes lie now,
Moulded in natural melancholy
Of untilled country, chin and cheek and brow.

The hour absorbs the players and the girl
10 Dreaming above the clematis. The ball
Coming and going weaves its spell,

And her eyes with the ball run to and fro.
Only the tracts of cheek and temple know
She has a long journey to go.

(1982)

YOUTH, AGE, AND DEATH: GROWING UP, GROWING OLD

My Father's Language

Leontia Flynn (b. 1974)

When my father sits in the straight-backed leather chair
the room contains him as my head contains this thought
of him. As though, in the gathering darkness,
made safe by the position of a rug or lamp
5   he is not being lost to shadows and incoherence.

As though he is not being lost to the drift of age.
Alzheimer's – slow accumulation of losses.
First, memory: the near shore of my father's life,
licked by the small waves, starts to grow faint and vague.
10   Next it is swept clear by the escaping tide.

First memory, then language. What process of attrition
('tangles', the text books answer, 'fatty plaques'[1])
sees him revert to a spoken Anglo-Saxon?
His language rattles in its dearth of nouns.
15   Everything is a 'thing'. 'Where is the thing for the thing?'

'Where is the thing? The thing, you know, the thing?'
(In this bone-dry wasteland where the nouns have died
'daughter' might sometimes be confused with 'wife'.)
I say: *The thing's not lost. No. Take this thing.*
20   *Here is the thing. The thing – Daddy – take this thing.*

(2011)

---

1 tangles ... fatty plaques terms taken from medical accounts of the causes of Alzheimer's disease

Piano

D.H. Lawrence (1885–1930)

Softly, in the dusk, a woman is singing to me;
Taking me back down the vista of years, till I see
A child sitting under the piano, in the boom of the
    tingling strings
5   And pressing the small, poised feet of a mother who smiles as
    she sings.

In spite of myself, the insidious mastery of song
Betrays me back, till the heart of me weeps to belong
To the old Sunday evenings at home, with winter outside
10 And hymns in the cosy parlour, the tinkling piano our guide.

So now it is vain for the singer to burst into clamour
With the great black piano appassionato[1]. The glamour
Of childish days is upon me, my manhood is cast
Down in the flood of remembrance, I weep like a child
15   for the past.

(1905–1907; published 1918)

---

1 appassionato with strong feeling (a technical musical term)

YOUTH, AGE, AND DEATH: GROWING UP, GROWING OLD

The Self-Unseeing

Thomas Hardy (1840–1928)

Here is the ancient floor,
Footworn and hollowed and thin,
Here was the former door
Where the dead feet walked in.

5 She sat here in her chair,
Smiling into the fire;
He who played stood there,
Bowing it higher and higher.

Childlike, I danced in a dream;
10 Blessings emblazoned that day;
Everything glowed with a gleam;
Yet we were looking away!

(1901)

Remembrance

Emily Jane Brontë (1818–1848)

Cold in the earth – and the deep snow piled above thee,
Far, far, removed, cold in the dreary grave!
Have I forgot, my only Love, to love thee,
Severed at last by Time's all-severing wave?

5 Now, when alone, do my thoughts no longer hover
Over the mountains, on that northern shore,
Resting their wings where heath and fern-leaves cover
Thy noble heart for ever, ever more?

Cold in the earth – and fifteen wild Decembers,
10 From those brown hills, have melted into spring:
Faithful, indeed, is the spirit that remembers
After such years of change and suffering!

Sweet Love of youth, forgive, if I forget thee,
While the world's tide is bearing me along;
15 Other desires and other hopes beset me,
Hopes which obscure, but cannot do thee wrong!

No later light has lightened up my heaven,
No second morn has ever shone for me;
All my life's bliss from thy dear life was given,
20 All my life's bliss is in the grave with thee.

But, when the days of golden dreams had perished,
And even Despair was powerless to destroy;
Then did I learn how existence could be cherished,
Strengthened, and fed without the aid of joy.

25 Then did I check the tears of useless passion –
Weaned my young soul from yearning after thine;
Sternly denied its burning wish to hasten
Down to that tomb already more than mine.

And, even yet, I dare not let it languish,
30 Dare not indulge in memory's rapturous pain;
Once drinking deep of that divinest anguish,
How could I seek the empty world again?

(1846)

Remember

Christina Rossetti (1830–1894)

Remember me when I am gone away,
    Gone far away into the silent land;
    When you can no more hold me by the hand,
Nor I half turn to go yet turning stay.
Remember me when no more day by day
    You tell me of our future that you plann'd:
    Only remember me; you understand
It will be late to counsel then or pray.
Yet if you should forget me for a while
    And afterwards remember, do not grieve:
    For if the darkness and corruption leave
A vestige of the thoughts that once I had,
Better by far you should forget and smile
    Than that you should remember and be sad.

(1849; published 1862)

Song

Christina Rossetti (1830–1894)

When I am dead, my dearest,
    Sing no sad songs for me;
Plant thou no roses at my head,
    Nor shady cypress tree:
5 Be the green grass above me
    With showers and dewdrops wet:
And if thou wilt, remember,
    And if thou wilt, forget.

I shall not see the shadows,
10   I shall not feel the rain;
I shall not hear the nightingale
    Sing on as if in pain:
And dreaming through the twilight
    That doth not rise nor set,
15 Haply I may remember,
    And haply may forget.

(1848; published 1862)

To an Athlete Dying Young

A.E. Housman (1859–1936)

The time you won your town the race
We chaired¹ you through the market-place;
Man and boy stood cheering by,
And home we brought you shoulder-high.

5   To-day, the road all runners come,
Shoulder-high we bring you home,
And set you at your threshold down,
Townsman of a stiller town.

Smart lad, to slip betimes away
10 From fields where glory does not stay
And early though the laurel grows
It withers quicker than the rose.

Eyes the shady night has shut
Cannot see the record cut,
15 And silence sounds no worse than cheers
After earth has stopped the ears:

Now you will not swell the rout
Of lads that wore their honours out,
Runners whom renown outran
20 And the name died before the man.

So set, before its echoes fade,
The fleet foot on the sill of shade,
And hold to the low lintel up
The still-defended challenge-cup.

25 And round that early-laurelled head
   Will flock to gaze the strengthless dead,
   And find unwithered on its curls
   The garland briefer than a girl's.

(1896)

---

1 chaired the winner of an important competition would be put in a chair and carried high in triumph by the celebrating crowd

Forefathers
Edmund Blunden (1896–1974)

Here they went with smock and crook,
    Toil'd in the sun, loll'd in the shade,
Here they muddled[1] out the brook
    And here their hatchet clear'd the glade:
5 Harvest-supper woke their wit,
Huntsman's moon their wooings lit.

From this church they led their brides,
    From this church themselves were led
Shoulder-high; on these waysides
10   Sat to take their beer and bread.
Names are gone—what men they were
These their cottages declare.

Names are vanish'd, save the few
    In the old brown Bible scrawl'd;
15 These were men of pith and thew[2]
    Whom the city never call'd;
Scarce could read or hold a quill,
Built the barn, the forge, the mill.

On the green they watch'd their sons
20   Playing till too dark to see,
As their fathers watch'd them once,
    As my father once watch'd me;
While the bat and beetle flew
On the warm air webb'd with dew.

Unrecorded, unrenown'd,
    Men from whom my ways begin,
Here I know you by your ground
    But I know you not within—
There is silence, there survives
Not a moment of your lives.

Like the bee that now is blown
    Honey-heavy on my hand,
From his toppling tansy[3]-throne
    In the green tempestuous land—
I'm in clover now, nor know
Who made honey long ago.

(1922)

---

1 muddled bathed or wallowed
2 pith and thew vigour and muscular strength
3 tansy a tall plant, such as silverweed or goose-grass

Going for the Milk

Mary Webb (1881–1927)

Going for the milk –
A toddling child with skin like curds,
On a May morning in a charm of birds:

Going for the milk
5   With laughing, teasing lads, at seventeen,
With rosy cheeks and breast as soft as silk –
Eh! what a mort[1] of years between!

Going for the milk
Through my Jim's garden, past the bush o'balm[2],
10   With my first baby sleeping on my arm:

It's fifty year, come Easter, since that day;
The work'us[3] ward is cold, my eyes be dim;
Never no more I'll go the flowery way,
Fetching the milk. I drink the pauper's skim[4],
15   And mind me of those summer days, and Jim
Telling me as my breast was soft as silk –
And that first day I missed to fetch the milk.

(1928)

---

1 **mort** a large quantity or number; it can also refer to a girl or young woman
2 **bush o'balm** a fragrant garden herb
3 **work'us** workhouse
4 **pauper's skim** milk after the rich cream has been taken off, which was the only kind of milk the poor could afford

YOUTH, AGE, AND DEATH: GROWING UP, GROWING OLD

Another and Another and Another

James Henry (1798–1876)

    Another and another and another
    And still another sunset and sunrise,
    The same yet different, different yet the same,
    Seen by me now in my declining years
5   As in my early childhood, youth and manhood;
    And by my parents and my parents' parents,
    And by the parents of my parents' parents,
    And by their parents counted back for ever,
    Seen, all their lives long, even as now by me;
10   And by my children and my children's children
    And by the children of my children's children
    And by their children counted on for ever
    Still to be seen as even now seen by me;
    Clear and bright sometimes, sometimes dark and clouded
15   But still the same sunsetting and sunrise;
    The same for ever to the never ending
    Line of observers, to the same observer
    Through all the changes of his life the same:
    Sunsetting and sunrising and sunsetting,
20   And then again sunrising and sunsetting,
    Sunrising and sunsetting evermore.

(1854)

anyone lived in a pretty how town

e.e. cummings (1894–1962)

anyone lived in a pretty how town
(with up so floating many bells down)
spring summer autumn winter
he sang his didn't he danced his did.

5   Women and men (both little and small)
cared for anyone not at all
they sowed their isn't they reaped their same
sun moon stars rain

children guessed (but only a few
10 and down they forgot as up they grew
autumn winter spring summer)
that noone loved him more by more

when by now and tree by leaf
she laughed his joy she cried his grief
15 bird by snow and stir by still
anyone's any was all to her

someones married their everyones
laughed their cryings and did their dance
(sleep wake hope and then) they
20 said their nevers they slept their dream

stars rain sun moon
(and only the snow can begin to explain
how children are apt to forget to remember
with up so floating many bells down)

25   one day anyone died i guess
(and noone stooped to kiss his face)
busy folk buried them side by side
little by little and was by was

all by all and deep by deep
30   and more by more they dream their sleep
noone and anyone earth by april
wish by spirit and if by yes.

Women and men (both dong and ding)
summer autumn winter spring
35   reaped their sowing and went their came
sun moon stars rain

                                                (1940)

Crossing the Bar

Alfred Tennyson (1809–1892)

Sunset and evening star,
   And one clear call for me!
And may there be no moaning of the bar[1],
   When I put out to sea,

5 But such a tide as moving seems asleep,
   Too full for sound and foam,
When that which drew from out the boundless deep
   Turns again home.

Twilight and evening bell,
10   And after that the dark!
And may there be no sadness of farewell,
   When I embark;

For tho' from out our bourne[2] of Time and Place
   The flood may bear me far,
15 I hope to see my Pilot[3] face to face
   When I have crost the bar.

(1889)

---

1 bar a bank of sand across the mouth of a harbour
2 bourne correctly, a limit or terminus; sometimes, as apparently here, used incorrectly to mean a domain or realm
3 Pilot a specialist navigator who takes a ship into and out of a port

Love, Family, and Relationships: The Bonds Between Us

The Rigs o' Barley

Robert Burns (1759–1796)

It was upon a Lammas night[1],
    When corn rigs[2] are bonie,
Beneath the moon's unclouded light,
    I held awa[3] to Annie:
5 The time flew by, wi' tentless[4] heed,
    Till 'tween the late and early;
Wi' sma' persuasion she agreed,
    To see me thro' the barley.

Chorus – Corn rigs, an' barley rigs,
10   An' corn rigs are bonie:
I'll ne'er forget that happy night,
    Amang the rigs wi' Annie.

The sky was blue, the wind was still,
    The moon was shining clearly;
15 I set her down, wi' right good will,
    Amang the rigs o' barley:
I ken't[5] her heart was a' my ain;
    I lov'd her most sincerely;
I kiss'd her owre[6] and owre again,
20   Amang the rigs o' barley.

Chorus

I lock'd her in my fond embrace;
    Her heart was beating rarely:
My blessings on that happy place,
25   Amang the rigs o' barley!
But by the moon and stars so bright,
    That shone that hour so clearly!
She ay shall bless that happy night,
    Amang the rigs o' barley.

30 *Chorus*

I hae been blythe wi' Comrades dear;
    I hae been merry drinking;
I hae been joyfu' gath'rin gear[7];
    I hae been happy thinking:
35 But a' the pleasures e'er I saw,
    Tho' three times doubl'd fairly,
That happy night was worth them a',
    Amang the rigs o' barley.

Chorus

(1786)

---

1 **Lammas night** a harvest festival celebrated on 1 August
2 **rigs** ridges
3 **awa** away
4 **tentless** careless
5 **ken't** knew
6 **owre** over
7 **gath'rin gear** making money

From Don Juan

George Gordon, Lord Byron (1788–1824)

> This excerpt is from a long poem recounting the adventures of its amiable hero, young Juan. At this point in the story (Canto II) Juan, having survived a disaster at sea, has been washed up on the shore of an unknown island, where he is looked after by a young woman, Haidee. They shortly fall in love, even though they are unable to understand one another's language.

183

It was the cooling hour, just when the rounded
    Red sun sinks down behind the azure[1] hill,
Which then seems as if the whole earth is bounded,
    Circling all nature, hush'd, and dim, and still,
With the far mountain-crescent half surrounded
    On one side, and the deep sea calm and chill
Upon the other, and the rosy sky,
With one star sparkling through it like an eye.

184

And thus they wander'd forth, and hand in hand,
    Over the shining pebbles and the shells,
Glided along the smooth and harden'd sand,
    And in the worn and wild receptacles
Work'd by the storms, yet work'd as it were plann'd,
    In hollow halls, with sparry roofs and cells,
They turn'd to rest; and, each clasp'd by an arm,
Yielded to the deep twilight's purple charm.

185

They look'd up to the sky, whose floating glow
   Spread like a rosy ocean, vast and bright;
They gazed upon the glittering sea below,
   Whence the broad moon rose circling into sight;
They heard the wave's splash, and the wind so low,
   And saw each other's dark eyes darting light
Into each other—and, beholding this,
Their lips drew near, and clung into a kiss;

186

A long, long kiss, a kiss of youth, and love,
   And beauty, all concentrating like rays
Into one focus, kindled from above;
   Such kisses as belong to early days,
Where heart, and soul, and sense, in concert move,
   And the blood's lava, and the pulse a blaze,
Each kiss a heart-quake,—for a kiss's strength,
I think, it must be reckon'd by its length.

187

By length I mean duration; theirs endured
   Heaven knows how long—no doubt they never reckon'd;
And if they had, they could not have secured
   The sum of their sensations to a second:
They had not spoken; but they felt allured,
   As if their souls and lips each other beckon'd,
Which, being join'd, like swarming bees they clung—
Their hearts the flowers from whence the honey sprung.

188

They were alone, but not alone as they
    Who shut in chambers think it loneliness;
The silent ocean, and the starlight bay,
    The twilight glow, which momently grew less,
45 The voiceless sands, and dropping caves, that lay
    Around them, made them to each other press,
As if there were no life beneath the sky
Save theirs, and that their life could never die.

189

They fear'd no eyes nor ears on that lone beach,
50   They felt no terrors from the night, they were
All in all to each other: though their speech
    Was broken words, they *thought* a language there,—
And all the burning tongues the passions teach
    Found in one sigh the best interpreter
55 Of nature's oracle—first love,—that all
Which Eve has left her daughters since her fall.

(1819)

---

1 azure a bright, clear blue; a poetical expression

LOVE, FAMILY, AND RELATIONSHIPS: THE BONDS BETWEEN US

From Sonnets from the Portuguese

Elizabeth Barrett Browning (1806–1861)

> This is number 14 in a sequence of poems that pretend to be translations: really, they were original English poems.

If thou must love me, let it be for nought
Except for love's sake only. Do not say,
"I love her for her smile…her look…her way
Of speaking gently, …for a trick of thought
5 That falls in well with mine, and certes[1] brought
A sense of pleasant ease on such a day"—
For these things in themselves, Beloved, may
Be changed, or change for thee,—and love so wrought,
May be unwrought so. Neither love me for
10 Thine own dear pity's wiping my cheeks dry,
Since one might well forget to weep who bore
Thy comfort long, and lose thy love thereby.
But love me for love's sake, that evermore
Thou may'st love on through love's eternity.

(1846; published 1850)

---

1 certes certainly

Meeting at Night

Robert Browning (1812–1889)

1

The grey sea and the long black land;
And the yellow half-moon large and low;
And the startled little waves that leap
In fiery ringlets from their sleep,
5   As I gain the cove with pushing prow,
And quench its speed i' the slushy sand.

2

Then a mile of warm sea-scented beach;
Three fields to cross till a farm appears;
A tap at the pane, the quick sharp scratch
10   And blue spurt of a lighted match,
And a voice less loud, thro' its joys and fears,
Than the two hearts beating each to each!

(1845)

LOVE, FAMILY, AND RELATIONSHIPS: THE BONDS BETWEEN US

The Miller's Daughter

Alfred Tennyson (1809–1892)

> This is part (lines 169–186) of a longer poem.

It is the miller's daughter,
   And she is grown so dear, so dear,
That I would be the jewel
   That trembles in her ear:
5 For hid in ringlets day and night,
I'd touch her neck so warm and white.

And I would be the girdle
   About her dainty dainty waist,
And her heart would beat against me,
10   In sorrow and in rest:
And I should know if it beat right,
I'd clasp it round so close and tight.

And I would be the necklace,
   And all day long to fall and rise
15 Upon her balmy bosom,
   With her laughter or her sighs,
And I would lie so light, so light,
I scarce should be unclasp'd at night.

(1832)

Love is Enough

William Morris (1834–1896)

Love is enough: though the World be a-waning,
And the woods have no voice but the voice of complaining,
   Though the sky be too dark for dim eyes to discover
The gold-cups and daisies fair blooming thereunder,
Though the hills be held shadows, and the sea a dark wonder
   And this day draw a veil over all deeds pass'd over,
Yet their hands shall not tremble, their feet shall not falter;
The void shall not weary, the fear shall not alter
   These lips and these eyes of the loved and the lover.

(1873)

LOVE, FAMILY, AND RELATIONSHIPS: THE BONDS BETWEEN US

Awake, my Heart, to be loved

Robert Bridges (1844–1930)

Awake, my heart, to be loved, awake, awake!
The darkness silvers away, the morn doth break,
It leaps in the sky: unrisen lustres slake
The o'ertaken moon. Awake, O heart, awake!

5   She too that loveth awaketh and hopes for thee;
Her eyes already have sped the shades that flee,
Already they watch the path thy feet shall take:
Awake, O heart, to be loved, awake, awake!

And if thou tarry from her,—if this could be,—
10 She cometh herself, O heart, to be loved, to thee;
For thee would unashamèd herself forsake:
Awake to be loved, my heart, awake, awake!

Awake, the land is scattered with light, and see,
Uncanopied sleep is flying from field and tree:
15 And blossoming boughs of April in laughter shake;
Awake, O heart, to be loved, awake, awake!

Lo all things wake and tarry and look for thee:
She looketh and saith, 'O sun, now bring him to me.
Come more adored, O adored, for his coming's sake,
20 And awake my heart to be loved: awake, awake!'

(1884)

Putting in the Seed
Robert Frost (1875–1963)

You come to fetch me from my work tonight
When supper's on the table, and we'll see
If I can leave off burying the white
Soft petals fallen from the apple tree
5   (Soft petals, yes, but not so barren quite,
Mingled with these, smooth bean and wrinkled pea;)
And go along with you ere you lose sight
Of what you came for and become like me,
Slave to a springtime passion for the earth.
10 How Love burns through the Putting in the Seed
On through the watching for that early birth
When, just as the soil tarnishes with weed,
The sturdy seedling with arched body comes
Shouldering its way and shedding the earth crumbs.

(1916)

Hinterhof

James Fenton (b. 1949)

Stay near to me and I'll stay near to you –
As near as you are dear to me will do,
   Near as the rainbow to the rain,
   The west wind to the windowpane,
As fire to the hearth, as dawn to dew.

Stay true to me and I'll stay true to you –
As true as you are new to me will do,
   New as the rainbow in the spray,
   Utterly new in every way,
New in the way that what you say is true.

Stay near to me, stay true to me. I'll stay
As near, as true to you as heart could pray.
   Heart never hoped that one might be
   Half of the things you are to me –
The dawn, the fire, the rainbow and the day.

(1994)

'Hinterhof' German for 'back courtyard'

Digging

Seamus Heaney (1939–2013)

Between my finger and my thumb
The squat pen rests; snug as a gun.

Under my window, a clean rasping sound
When the spade sinks into gravelly ground:
My father, digging. I look down

Till his straining rump among the flowerbeds
Bends low, comes up twenty years away
Stooping in rhythm through potato drills[1]
Where he was digging.

The coarse boot nestled on the lug[2], the shaft
Against the inside knee was levered firmly.
He rooted out tall tops, buried the bright edge deep
To scatter new potatoes that we picked
Loving their cool hardness in our hands.

By God, the old man could handle a spade.
Just like his old man.

My grandfather cut more turf in a day
Than any other man on Toner's bog.
Once I carried him milk in a bottle
Corked sloppily with paper. He straightened up
To drink it, then fell to right away
Nicking and slicing neatly, heaving sods[3]
Over his shoulder, going down and down
For the good turf. Digging.

25 The cold smell of potato mould, the squelch and slap
   Of soggy peat, the curt cuts of an edge
   Through living roots awaken in my head.
   But I've no spade to follow men like them.

   Between my finger and my thumb
30 The squat pen rests.
   I'll dig with it.

                                                    (1966)

---

1 drills furrows in soil in which seeds are planted
2 lug the shoulder of a spade on which the foot is placed when digging
3 sods slices of earth and grass

Praise Song for My Mother

Grace Nichols (b. 1950)

You were
water to me
deep and bold and fathoming

You were
moon's eye to me
pull and grained and mantling

You were
sunrise to me
rise and warm and streaming

You were
the fishes red gill to me
the flame tree's spread to me
the crab's leg/the fried plantain smell
          replenishing replenishing

Go to your wide futures, you said

(1984)

Clearing I

Tony Harrison (b. 1937)

The ambulance, the hearse, the auctioneers
clear all the life of that loved house away.
The hard-earned treasures of some 50 years
sized up as junk, and shifted in a day.

5 A stammerer died here and I believe
this front room with such ghosts taught me my trade.
Now strangers chip the paintwork as they heave
the spotless piano that was never played.
The fingerprints they leave mam won't wipe clean
10 nor politely ask them first to wipe their boots,
nor coax her trampled soil patch back to green
after they've trodden down the pale spring shoots.

I'd hope my mother's spirit wouldn't chase
her scattered household, even if it could.
15 How could she bear it when she saw no face
stare back at her from that long polished wood?

(1978)

Aunt Julia

Norman MacCaig (1910–1996)

Aunt Julia spoke Gaelic
very loud and very fast.
I could not answer her –
I could not understand her.

5   She wore men's boots
when she wore any.
– I can see her strong foot,
stained with peat,
paddling with the treadle of the spinningwheel
10   while her right hand drew yarn
marvellously out of the air.

Hers was the only house
where I've lain at night
in the absolute darkness
15   of a box bed, listening to
crickets being friendly.

She was buckets
and water flouncing into them.
She was winds pouring wetly
20   round house-ends.
She was brown eggs, black skirts
and a keeper of threepennybits
in a teapot.

Aunt Julia spoke Gaelic
25 very loud and very fast.
By the time I had learned
a little, she lay
silenced in the absolute black
of a sandy grave
30 at Luskentyre. But I hear her still, welcoming me
with a seagull's voice
across a hundred yards
of peatscrapes and lazybeds
and getting angry, getting angry
35 with so many questions
unanswered.

(1968)

For my Niece

Kate Tempest (b. 1985)

I hold you in my arms,
your age is told in months.

There's things I hope you'll learn.
Things I'm sure I learned once.

5   But there's nothing I can teach you.
You'll find all that you need.

No flower bends its head to offer
teaching to a seed.

The seed will grow and blossom
10 once the flower's ground to dust.

But even so, if nothing else,
one thing I'll entrust:

Doing what you please
is not the same

15 as doing what you must.

(2014)

Poem

Simon Armitage (b. 1963)

And if it snowed and snow covered the drive
he took a spade and tossed it to one side.
And always tucked his daughter up at night.
And slippered her the one time that she lied.

And every week he tipped up half his wage.
And what he didn't spend each week he saved.
And praised his wife for every meal she made.
And once, for laughing, punched her in the face.

And for his mum he hired a private nurse.
And every Sunday taxied her to church.
And he blubbed when she went from bad to worse.
And twice he lifted ten quid from her purse.

Here's how they rated him when they looked back:
sometimes he did this, sometimes he did that.

(1992)

When the Lamp is Shattered

Percy Bysshe Shelley (1792–1822)

    When the lamp is shatter'd,
The light in the dust lies dead;
    When the cloud is scatter'd,
The rainbow's glory is shed;
5   When the lute is broken,
Sweet tones are remember'd not;
    When the lips have spoken,
Loved accents are soon forgot.

    As music and splendour
10 Survive not the lamp and the lute,
    The heart's echoes render
No song when the spirit is mute—
    No song but sad dirges,
Like the wind through a ruin'd cell,
15   Or the mournful surges
That ring the dead seaman's knell.

    When hearts have once mingled,
Love first leaves the well-built nest;
    The weak one is singled
20 To endure what it once possest.
    O Love, who bewailest
The frailty of all things here,
    Why choose you the frailest
For your cradle, your home, and your bier[1]?

25   Its passions will rock thee,
      As the storms rock the ravens on high:
        Bright reason will mock thee,
    Like the sun from a wintry sky.
        From thy nest every rafter
30   Will rot, and thine eagle home
        Leave thee naked to laughter,
    When leaves fall and cold winds come.

(1821–1822)

---

1 bier the stand on which a corpse is laid before it is buried

Love's Secret

William Blake (1757–1827)

> This title is not Blake's but the work of his Victorian editor: the original poem, which contains many crossings-out and may not be finished, exists only in manuscript, where it has no title.

Never seek to tell thy love,
   Love that never told can be;
For the gentle wind does move
   Silently, invisibly.

5 I told my love, I told my love,
   I told her all my heart,
Trembling, cold, in ghastly fears.
   Ah! she did depart!

Soon after she was gone from me,
10   A traveller came by,
Silently, invisibly:
   He took her with a sigh.

(c.1793; published 1863)

In Drear-Nighted December

John Keats (1795–1821)

In drear-nighted December,
    Too happy, happy tree,
Thy Branches ne'er remember
    Their green felicity[1]:
5 The north cannot undo them,
    With a sleety whistle through them;
Nor frozen thawings glue them
    From budding at the prime.

In drear-nighted December,
10   Too happy, happy Brook,
Thy bubblings ne'er remember
    Apollo's[2] summer look;
But with a sweet forgetting,
They stay their crystal fretting,
15 Never, never petting
    About the frozen time.

Ah! would 'twere so with many
    A gentle girl and boy!
But were there ever any
20   Writh'd not of passed joy?
The feel of not to feel it,
When there is none to heal it,
Nor numbed sense to steel it,
    Was never said in rhyme.

(1817; published 1829)

---

1 felicity happiness
2 Apollo in ancient myth, the god of poetry, music, and healing

À Quoi Bon Dire

Charlotte Mew (1869–1928)

Seventeen years ago you said
    Something that sounded like Good-bye;
    And everybody thinks that you are dead,
        But I.

5   So I, as I grow stiff and cold
To this and that say Good-bye too;
    And everybody sees that I am old
        But you.

    And one fine morning in a sunny lane
10 Some boy and girl will meet and kiss and swear
    That nobody can love their way again
        While over there
You will have smiled, I shall have tossed your hair.

(1921)

À Quoi Bon Dire what's the good of saying

LOVE, FAMILY, AND RELATIONSHIPS: THE BONDS BETWEEN US

The rain, it streams on stone and hillock

A.E. Housman (1859–1936)

The rain, it streams on stone and hillock,
    The boot clings to the clay.
Since all is done that's due and right
Let's home; and now, my lad, good-night,
    For I must turn away.

Good-night, my lad, for nought's eternal;
    No league of ours, for sure.
To-morrow I shall miss you less,
And ache of heart and heaviness
    Are things that time should cure.

Over the hill the highway marches
    And what's beyond is wide:
Oh soon enough will pine to nought
Remembrance and the faithful thought
    That sits the grave beside.

The skies, they are not always raining
    Nor grey the twelvemonth through;
And I shall meet good days and mirth,
And range the lovely lands of earth
    With friends no worse than you.

But oh, my man, the house is fallen
    That none can build again;
My man, how full of joy and woe
Your mother bore you years ago
    To-night to lie in the rain.

(1899–1922; published 1922)

Auld Lang Syne

Robert Burns (1759–1796)

Should auld acquaintance be forgot
    And never brought to mind?
Should auld acquaintance be forgot,
    And auld lang syne!

5 *Chorus* – For auld lang syne my jo,
For auld lang syne,
We'll tak a cup o' kindness yet
For auld lang syne.

And surely ye'll be your pint stowp!
10   And surely I'll be mine!
And we'll tak a cup o' kindness yet,
    For auld lang syne.

Chorus

We twa hae run about the braes,
    And pou'd the gowans fine;
15 But we've wander'd mony a weary fitt,
    Sin auld lang syne.

Chorus

We twa hae paidl'd in the burn,
    Frae morning sun till dine;
But seas between us braid hae roar'd,
20   Sin auld lang syne.

Chorus

And there's a hand, my trusty fiere!
   And gie's a hand o' thine!
And we'll tak a right gude-willie-waught,
   For auld lang syne.

Chorus

(1788)

You Can't Take My World from Me
Tracey Herd (b. 1968)

Why did you give no warning? You got up to go
and left me here with the music, alone.
No please, I really don't want to know.

Doors slam. I have locked every window.
5 My heart echoes in an empty mansion
asking over and over, why did you go?

Well, you can't take my world with you.
I have decided to turn my heart into stone
because I really don't ever desire to know.

10 The lilies bloom; those skies, the sun's glow:
I have chiselled my final question
on the tiny white stone. Why did you go?

The sunset is beautiful, the darkness slow,
oh I have cut myself to the very bone
15 and I simply don't want to know.

I've left you now with the script you'll follow
so you will never forget what you've done.
You will never black out your decision to go.

And as for the reason, I will never know.

(2015)

Wild Things and Natural Places: The World Around Us

Open Winter
John Clare (1793–1864)

Where slanting banks are always with the sun
    The daisy is in blossom even now;
And where warm patches by the hedges run
    The cottager when coming home from plough
5 Brings home a cowslip root in flower to set.
Thus ere the Christmas goes the spring is met
    Setting up little tents about the fields
In sheltered spots.—Primroses, when they get
    Behind the wood's old roots, where ivy shields
10 Their crimpled, curdled leaves, will shine and hide.
—Cart-ruts and horses' footings scarcely yield
    A slur for boys, just crizzled[1] and that's all.
Frost shoots his needles by the small dyke side,
    And snow in scarce a feather's seen to fall.

(between 1832 and 1837; published 1935)

---

1 crizzled roughened and crisped, like water beginning to freeze

The Trees

Philip Larkin (1922–1985)

The trees are coming into leaf
Like something almost being said;
The recent buds relax and spread,
Their greenness is a kind of grief.

5 Is it that they are born again
And we grow old? No, they die too.
Their yearly trick of looking new
Is written down in rings of grain.

Yet still the unresting castles thresh
10 In fullgrown thickness every May.
Last year is dead, they seem to say,
Begin afresh, afresh, afresh.

(1967; published 1974)

The Death of Autumn

Edna St. Vincent Millay (1892–1950)

    When reeds are dead and a straw to thatch the marshes,
    And feathered pampas-grass rides into the wind
    Like agèd warriors westward, tragic, thinned
    Of half their tribe, and over the flattened rushes,
5   Stripped of its secret, open, stark and bleak,
    Blackens afar the half-forgotten creek,—
    Then leans on me the weight of the year, and crushes
    My heart. I know that Beauty must ail and die,
    And will be born again,—but ah, to see
10 Beauty stiffened, staring up at the sky!
    Oh, Autumn! Autumn!—What is the Spring to me?

(1921)

First Sight

Philip Larkin (1922–1985)

Lambs that learn to walk in snow
When their bleating clouds the air
Meet a vast unwelcome, know
Nothing but a sunless glare.
Newly stumbling to and fro
All they find, outside the fold,
Is a wretched width of cold.

As they wait beside the ewe,
Her fleeces wetly caked, there lies
Hidden round them, waiting too,
Earth's immeasurable surprise.
They could not grasp it if they knew,
What so soon will wake and grow
Utterly unlike the snow.

(1956; published 1964)

The Darkling Thrush

Thomas Hardy (1840–1928)

> Despite the date that Hardy himself attaches to it, this poem was first published on 29 December 1900 under the title 'By the Century's Deathbed'.

I leant upon a coppice gate
   When Frost was spectre-gray,
And Winter's dregs made desolate
   The weakening eye of day.
5 The tangled bine-stems scored the sky
   Like strings of broken lyres,
And all mankind that haunted nigh
   Had sought their household fires.

The land's sharp features seemed to be
10   The Century's corpse outleant,
His crypt the cloudy canopy,
   The wind his death-lament.
The ancient pulse of germ and birth
   Was shrunken hard and dry,
15 And every spirit upon earth
   Seemed fervourless as I.

At once a voice arose among
   The bleak twigs overhead
In a full-hearted evensong
20   Of joy illimited;
An aged thrush, frail, gaunt, and small,
   In blast-beruffled plume,
Had chosen thus to fling his soul
   Upon the growing gloom.

25 So little cause for carolings
    Of such ecstatic sound
Was written on terrestrial things
    Afar or nigh around,
That I could think there trembled through
30   His happy good-night air
Some blessed Hope, whereof he knew
    And I was unaware.

                (31 December 1900)

The Robin in Autumn

Bernard O'Donoghue (b. 1945)

    He's watched the prizewinners,
    One by one, taking off
    For their world tour, until
    At last he's top of the bill.
5 Without the competition
    Of the blackcap, his lyric
    From the leaves is as good
    As anyone's, even becoming
    Indistinguishable from the champions
10 In the ear's memory. In due course
    The leaves themselves will fly
    And he'll stand out alone
    On the bare rostrum
    Of his Christmas card.

(1995)

Cabbage Dreams

Jo Shapcott (b. 1953)

    After dark, cabbages are proud and brilliant,
    supercool. We stalk the garden
    under the moon discussing politics with flowers.
    We inspect your houses in the early hours
5 criticising the curtains, wondering about
    the furniture, amazed at your reading habits.
    Your clothes baffle us though we know
    about layers and the colour of leaves.
    We stare at your flabby fingers while
10 you sleep, speculate about your hairstyles.
    Daytimes we fall back into ourselves,
    sit around in vegetable racks, clutch
    stubby leaves round our green shoulders
    and hope you remember our sweet hearts.

(1998)

Snake

D.H. Lawrence (1885–1930)

A snake came to my water-trough
On a hot, hot day, and I in pyjamas for the heat,
To drink there.

In the deep, strange-scented shade of the great dark carob
5   tree
I came down the steps with my pitcher
And must wait, must stand and wait, for there he was at the
   trough before me.

He reached down from a fissure in the earth-wall
10   in the gloom
And trailed his yellow-brown slackness soft-bellied down,
   over the edge of the stone trough
And rested his throat upon the stone bottom,
And where the water had dripped from the tap, in a small
15   clearness,
He sipped with his straight mouth,
Softly drank through his straight gums, into his slack long
   body,
Silently.

20 Someone was before me at my water-trough,
And I, like a second-comer, waiting.

He lifted his head from his drinking, as cattle do,
And looked at me vaguely, as drinking cattle do,
And flickered his two-forked tongue from his lips, and
25   mused a moment,
And stooped and drank a little more,

Being earth-brown, earth-golden from the burning bowels
   of the earth
On the day of Sicilian July, with Etna[1] smoking.

30 The voice of my education said to me
He must be killed,
For in Sicily the black, black snakes are innocent, the gold
   are venomous.

And voices in me said, If you were a man
35 You would take a stick and break him now, and finish him off.

But must I confess how I liked him,
How glad I was he had come like a guest in quiet, to drink at
   my water-trough
And depart peaceful, pacified, and thankless
40 Into the burning bowels of this earth?

Was it cowardice, that I dared not kill him?
Was it perversity, that I longed to talk to him?
Was it humility, to feel so honoured?
I felt so honoured.

45 And yet those voices:
If you were not afraid, you would kill him!

And truly I was afraid, I was most afraid,
But even so, honoured still more
That he should seek my hospitality
50 From out the dark door of the secret earth.

He drank enough
And lifted his head, dreamily, as one who has drunken,
And flickered his tongue like a forked night on the
   air, so black,

55 Seeming to lick his lips,
And looked around like a god, unseeing, into the air,
And slowly turned his head,
And slowly, very slowly, as if thrice adream
Proceeded to draw his slow length curving round
60 And climb again the broken bank of my wall-face.

And as he put his head into that dreadful hole,
And as he slowly drew up, snake-easing his shoulders, and entered further,
A sort of horror, a sort of protest against his withdrawing into
65   that horrid black hole,
Deliberately going into the blackness, and slowly drawing himself after,
Overcame me now his back was turned.

I looked round, I put down my pitcher,
70 I picked up a clumsy log
And threw it at the water-trough with a clatter.

I think it did not hit him;
But suddenly that part of him that was left behind convulsed in undignified haste,
75 Writhed like lightning, and was gone
Into the black hole, the earth-lipped fissure in the wall-front
At which, in the intense still noon, I stared with fascination.

And immediately I regretted it.
80 I thought how paltry, how vulgar, what a mean act!
I despised myself and the voices of my accursèd human education.

And I thought of the albatross[2],
And I wished he would come back, my snake.

85 For he seemed to me again like a king,
Like a king in exile, uncrowned in the underworld,
Now due to be crowned again.

And so, I missed my chance with one of the lords
Of life.
90 And I have something to expiate[3]:
A pettiness.

(1921)

---

1 **Etna** a volcano on the island of Sicily, where the poem is set
2 **albatross** an albatross, a great sea-bird, is cruelly killed in 'The Ancient Mariner', a poem by Samuel Taylor Coleridge
3 **to expiate** to confess and relieve yourself of a sin or a crime

The Snake

Emily Dickinson (1830–1886)

A narrow Fellow in the Grass
Occasionally rides –
You may have met Him – did you not
His notice sudden is –

5   The Grass divides as with a Comb –
A spotted shaft is seen –
And then it closes at your feet
And opens further on –

He likes a Boggy Acre
10 A Floor too cool for Corn –
Yet when a Boy, and Barefoot –
I more than once at Noon
Have passed, I thought, a Whip lash
Unbraiding[1] in the Sun
15 When stooping to secure it
It wrinkled, and was gone –

Several of Nature's People
I know, and they know me –
I feel for them a transport
20 Of cordiality –

But never met this Fellow
Attended, or alone
Without a tighter breathing
And Zero at the Bone –

(1865; published 1891)

---

1 Unbraiding separating the strands of something plaited

WILD THINGS AND NATURAL PLACES: THE WORLD AROUND US

The Fish

Elizabeth Bishop (1911–1979)

I caught a tremendous fish
and held him beside the boat
half out of water, with my hook
fast in a corner of his mouth.
5 He didn't fight.
He hadn't fought at all.
He hung a grunting weight,
battered and venerable
and homely. Here and there
10 his brown skin hung in strips
like ancient wallpaper,
and its pattern of darker brown
was like wallpaper:
shapes like full-blown roses
15 stained and lost through age.
He was speckled with barnacles,
fine rosettes of lime,
and infested
with tiny white sea-lice,
20 and underneath two or three
rags of green weed hung down.
While his gills were breathing in
the terrible oxygen
—the frightening gills,
25 fresh and crisp with blood,
that can cut so badly—
I thought of the coarse white flesh
packed in like feathers,
the big bones and the little bones,
30 the dramatic reds and blacks

of his shiny entrails,
and the pink swim-bladder
like a big peony.
I looked into his eyes
35 which were far larger than mine
but shallower, and yellowed,
the irises backed and packed
with tarnished tinfoil
seen through the lenses
40 of old scratched isinglass[1].
They shifted a little, but not
to return my stare.
—It was more like the tipping
of an object toward the light.
45 I admired his sullen face,
the mechanism of his jaw,
and then I saw
that from his lower lip
—if you could call it a lip—
50 grim, wet, and weaponlike,
hung five old pieces of fish-line,
or four and a wire leader
with the swivel still attached,
with all their five big hooks
55 grown firmly in his mouth.
A green line, frayed at the end
where he broke it, two heavier lines,
and a fine black thread
still crimped from the strain and snap
60 when it broke and he got away.
Like medals with their ribbons
frayed and wavering,
a five-haired beard of wisdom
trailing from his aching jaw.
65 I stared and stared

and victory filled up
the little rented boat,
from the pool of bilge[2]
where oil had spread a rainbow
70 around the rusted engine
to the bailer rusted orange,
the sun-cracked thwarts[3],
the oarlocks on their strings,
the gunnels[4]—until everything
75 was rainbow, rainbow, rainbow!
And I let the fish go.

(1946)

---

1 isinglass a semi-transparent substance, derived from fish, used in cooking
2 bilge the dirty water that collects in the bottom of a boat
3 thwarts the seats in a boat on which the rowers sit
4 gunnels the upper edge of a boat's side

To A Mouse

Robert Burns (1759–1796)

On turning her up in her Nest, with the Plough, November, 1785.

Wee, sleeket, cowran[1], tim'rous *beastie*,
O, what a panic's in thy breastie[2]!
Thou need na start awa sae hasty,
    Wi' bickering brattle[3]!
5   I wad be laith[4] to rin[5] an' chase thee,
    Wi' murd'ring *pattle*[6]!

  I'm truly sorry Man's dominion
Has broken Nature's social union,
An' justifies that ill opinion,
10   Which makes thee startle,
At me, thy poor, earth-born companion,
    An' *fellow-mortal!*

  I doubt na, whyles, but thou may *thieve*;
What then? poor beastie, thou maun live!
15   A *daimen-icker* in a *thrave*[7]
    'S a sma' request:
I'll get a blessin wi' the lave[8],
    An' never miss't!

  Thy wee-bit *housie*, too, in ruin!
20   It's silly[9] wa's the win's[10] are strewin!
An' naething, now, to big[11] a new ane,
    O' foggage[12] green!
An' bleak *December's winds* ensuin,
    Baith snell an' keen[13]!

25   Thou saw the fields laid bare an' wast[14],
An' weary *Winter* comin fast,

An' cozie here, beneath the blast,
    Thou thought to dwell,
Till crash! the cruel *coulter*[15] past
30   Out thro' thy cell.

  That wee-bit heap o' leaves an' stibble[16],
Has cost thee monie a weary nibble!
Now thou's turn'd out, for a' thy trouble,
    But house or hald[17],
35 To thole[18] the Winter's *sleety dribble*,
    An' *cranreuch* cauld[19]!

  But Mousie, thou are no thy-lane[20],
In proving *foresight* may be vain:
The best laid schemes o' *Mice* an' *Men*,
40   Gang aft agley[21],
An' lea'e us nought but grief an' pain,
    For promis'd joy!

  Still, thou art blest, compar'd wi' *me*!
The *present* only toucheth thee:
45 But Och! I *backward* cast my e'e,
    On prospects drear!
An' *forward*, tho' I canna *see*,
    I *guess* an' *fear*!

(1786)

---

1 **Wee, sleeket, cowran** little, sleek, fearful
2 **breastie** little breast
3 **bickering brattle** the sound of scampering
4 **laith** loath, reluctant
5 **rin** run
6 *pattle* plough staff
7 *daimen-icker* in a *thrave* the occasional ear of wheat from a bundle of sheaves
8 **lave** what's left
9 **silly** flimsy, frail
10 **win's** winds
11 **big** build
12 **foggage** rough grass growing between crops
13 **Baith snell an' keen** both bitter and sharp
14 **wast** waste
15 *coulter* the iron blade of the plough
16 **stibble** stubble
17 **But house or hald** without house or resting place
18 **thole** endure
19 *cranreuch cauld* cold frost
20 **no thy-lane** not alone
21 **Gang aft agley** often go awry

The Lamb

William Blake (1757–1827)

Little Lamb, who made thee?
Dost thou know who made thee?
Gave thee life, & bid thee feed
By the stream & o'er the mead;
Gave thee clothing of delight,
Softest clothing, wooly, bright;
Gave thee such a tender voice,
Making all the vales rejoice?
    Little Lamb, who made thee?
    Dost thou know who made thee?

    Little Lamb, I'll tell thee,
    Little Lamb, I'll tell thee:
He is called by thy name,
For he calls himself a Lamb[1].
He is meek, & he is mild;

He became a little child.
I a child, & thou a lamb,
We are called by his name.
    Little Lamb, God bless thee!
    Little Lamb, God bless thee!

(1789)

---

1 he calls himself a Lamb in the Bible, Jesus is described (by John the Baptist) as 'the Lamb of God, that taketh away the sin of the world' (John, 1:29)

The Tyger

William Blake (1757–1827)

Tyger! Tyger! burning bright
In the forests of the night,
What immortal hand or eye
Could frame thy fearful symmetry?

5   In what distant deeps or skies
Burnt the fire of thine eyes?
On what wings dare he aspire?
What the hand dare seize the fire?

And what shoulder, & what art,
10 Could twist the sinews of thy heart?
And when thy heart began to beat,
What dread hand? & what dread feet?

What the hammer? what the chain?
In what furnace was thy brain?
15 What the anvil? what dread grasp
Dare its deadly terrors clasp?

When the stars threw down their spears,
And water'd heaven with their tears,
Did he smile his work to see?
20 Did he who made the Lamb make thee?

Tyger! Tyger! burning bright
In the forests of the night,
What immortal hand or eye
Dare frame thy fearful symmetry?

(1794)

White-Sided Dolphins

Kathleen Jamie (b. 1962)

When there was no doubt,
no mistaking for water-glint
their dorsal fins'
urgent cut and dive

5 we grabbed cameras, threw ourselves
flat on the fore-deck. Then,
just for a short time
we travelled as one

loose formation: the muscular
10 wingers, mothers-with-young,
old scarred outriders
all breached alongside,

took it in turn
to swoon up through our pressure-wave,
15 careen[1] and appraise us
with a speculative eye

till they'd seen enough,
when true to their own
inner oceanic maps, the animals
20 veered off from us, north by northwest.

(2004)

---

1 careen to turn a boat over on its side in order to clean or repair the hull

The Jaguar

Ted Hughes (1930–1998)

The apes yawn and adore their fleas in the sun.
The parrots shriek as if they were on fire, or strut
Like cheap tarts to attract the stroller with the nut.
Fatigued with indolence, tiger and lion

Lie still as the sun. The boa-constrictor's coil
Is a fossil. Cage after cage seems empty, or
Stinks of sleepers from the breathing straw.
It might be painted on a nursery wall.

But who runs like the rest past these arrives
At a cage where the crowd stands, stares, mesmerized,
As a child at a dream, at a jaguar hurrying enraged
Through prison darkness after the drills of his eyes

On a short fierce fuse. Not in boredom—
The eye satisfied to be blind in fire,
By the bang of blood in the brain deaf the ear—
He spins from the bars, but there's no cage to him

More than to the visionary his cell:
His stride is wildernesses of freedom:
The world rolls under the long thrust of his heel.
Over the cage floor the horizons come.

(1957)

The Eagle
Alfred Tennyson (1809–1892)

He clasps the crag with crooked hands;
Close to the sun in lonely lands,
Ring'd with the azure world, he stands.

The wrinkled sea beneath him crawls;
5   He watches from his mountain walls,
And like a thunderbolt he falls.

(1849; published 1851)

WILD THINGS AND NATURAL PLACES: THE WORLD AROUND US

The Kraken
Alfred Tennyson (1809–1892)

> The kraken is a legendary sea creature of huge size, reputed to rise to the surface of the water only once, at which point it would perish.

Below the thunders of the upper deep;
Far, far beneath in the abysmal sea,
His ancient, dreamless, uninvaded sleep
The Kraken sleepeth: faintest sunlights flee
About his shadowy sides: above him swell
Huge sponges of millennial growth and height;
And far away into the sickly light,
From many a wondrous grot and secret cell
Unnumber'd and enormous polypi[1]
Winnow[2] with giant arms the slumbering green.
There hath he lain for ages and will lie
Battening upon huge seaworms in his sleep,
Until the latter fire shall heat the deep;
Then once by man and angels to be seen,
In roaring he shall rise and on the surface die.

(1830)

---

1 polypi sea creatures with tentacles
2 winnow to wave and flap the arms (or, here, tentacles)

Jabberwocky

'Lewis Carroll' [Charles Lutwidge Dodgson] (1832–1898)

> This poem appears in *Through the Looking-Glass, and What Alice Found There* (1871), the sequel to *Alice in Wonderland*. In chapter one, Alice comes across the text of the poem written in mirror-writing. She deciphers it by reading it in a mirror, but ends little wiser: '"It seems very pretty," she said when she had finished it, "but it's rather hard to understand!" (You see she didn't like to confess, even to herself, that she couldn't make it out at all.) "Somehow it seems to fill my head with ideas—only I don't exactly know what they are! However, somebody killed something: that's clear, at any rate—"'.

'Twas brillig, and the slithy toves
    Did gyre and gimble in the wabe:
All mimsy were the borogoves,
    And the mome raths outgrabe.

5 "Beware the Jabberwock, my son!
    The jaws that bite, the claws that catch!
Beware the Jubjub bird, and shun
    The frumious Bandersnatch!"

He took his vorpal sword in hand:
10   Long time the manxome foe he sought—
So rested he by the Tumtum tree,
    And stood awhile in thought.

And, as in uffish thought he stood,
    The Jabberwock, with eyes of flame,
15 Came whiffling through the tulgey wood,
    And burbled as it came!

One, two! One, two! And through and through
   The vorpal blade went snicker-snack!
He left it dead, and with its head
20   He went galumphing back.

"And hast thou slain the Jabberwock?
   Come to my arms, my beamish boy!
O frabjous day! Callooh! Callay!"
   He chortled in his joy.

25 'Twas brillig, and the slithy toves
    Did gyre and gimble in the wabe:
All mimsy were the borogoves,
   And the mome raths outgrabe.

(1871)

Squirrel's the Word

Sophie Hannah (b. 1971)

They're rats with bushy tails, you claim.
They bite and spread disease.
Despite the reassuring name
Of squirrel, they are wild, not tame,
5   *And they belong in trees.*

But there's a squirrel that I know
Who calls each day at nine,
Catches the croissant that I throw
And chomps it on the patio.
10 I think of him as mine.

He is both patient and polite
While I prepare his meal.
Squirrel's the word and it's the right
Word in his case, in fact he's quite
15 The squirrelish ideal,

So deconstruct him all you please
To bushy tail and rat.
Squirrel is still the name for these
Creatures with squirrels' qualities
20 And he is just like that.

(2003)

Bad Day at the Ark

Roger McGough (b. 1937)

On the eleventh morning
Japheth burst into the cabin:
'Dreadful news, everybody, the tigers
have eaten the bambanolas!'

5 'Oh, not the bambanolas,' cried Mrs Noah.
'But they were my favourites,
all cuddly and furry,
and such beautiful brown eyes.'

Noah took her hand in his.
10 'Momma, not only were they cute
but they could sing and dance
and speak seven languages.'

'And when baked, their dung was delicious,'
added Shem wistfully.
15 Everybody agreed that the earth
would be a poorer place without the bambanolas.

Noah determined to look on the bright side.
'At least we still have the quinquasaurapods.'
'Oh, yes, the darling creatures,' said his wife.
20 'How would we manage without them?'

On deck, one quinquasaurapod was steering,
cooking, fishing, doing a crossword
and finding a cure for cancer.
The other was being stalked by a tiger.

(1999)

Pied Beauty

Gerard M. Hopkins (1844–1899)

Glory be to God for dappled things—
   For skies of couple-colour as a brinded[1] cow;
      For rose-moles all in stipple upon trout that swim;
Fresh-firecoal chestnut-falls; finches' wings;
   Landscape plotted and pieced—fold, fallow[2], and plough;
      And áll trádes[3], their gear and tackle and trim.

All things counter, original, spare, strange;
   Whatever is fickle[4], freckled (who knows how?)
      With swift, slow; sweet, sour; adazzle, dim;
He fathers-forth whose beauty is past change:
                    Praise him.

                          (1877; published 1918)

Pied dappled, speckled
1 **brinded** brownish and streaked with different colours
2 **fallow** a reddish yellow colour, like a fallow deer
3 **áll trádes** the marks above these words are the author's, requiring the reader to stress the syllables in question
4 **fickle** changeable

Power, Conflict, and Violence: Inflicted Harms

After Blenheim

Robert Southey (1774–1843)

> The battle of Blenheim was fought in Bavaria on 13 August 1704, between British, Austrian, and Dutch troops on the one side, and French and Bavarian on the other. The British-led forces, commanded by the Duke of Marlborough, won a resounding victory, assisted by the arrival of Austrian troops commanded by Prince Eugene of Savoy. There were many casualties.

1

It was a summer evening,
   Old Kaspar's work was done,
And he before his cottage door
   Was sitting in the sun,
And by him sported on the green
His little grandchild Wilhelmine.

2

She saw her brother Peterkin
   Roll something large and round,
Which he beside the rivulet
   In playing there had found;
He came to ask what he had found,
That was so large, and smooth, and round.

3

Old Kaspar took it from the boy,
   Who stood expectant by;
And then the old man shook his head,
   And, with a natural sigh,
   ' 'Tis some poor fellow's skull,' said he,
'Who fell in the great victory.

4

'I find them in the garden,
    For there's many here about;
And often when I go to plough,
    The ploughshare turns them out!
For many thousand men,' said he,
    'Were slain in that great victory.'

5

'Now tell us what 'twas all about,'
    Young Peterkin, he cries;
And little Wilhelmine looks up
    With wonder-waiting eyes;
'Now tell us all about the war,
And what they fought each other for.'

6

'It was the English,' Kaspar cried,
    'Who put the French to rout;
But what they fought each other for,
    I could not well make out;
But everybody said,' quoth he,
'That 'twas a famous victory.

7

'My father lived at Blenheim then,
    Yon little stream hard by;
They burnt his dwelling to the ground,
    And he was forced to fly;
So with his wife and child he fled,
Nor had he where to rest his head.

8

'With fire and sword the country round
   Was wasted far and wide,
45 And many a childing mother then,
   And new-born baby died;
But things like that, you know, must be
At every famous victory.

9

'They say it was a shocking sight
50   After the field was won;
For many thousand bodies here
   Lay rotting in the sun;
But things like that, you know, must be
After a famous victory.

10

55 'Great praise the Duke of Marlbro' won,
   And our good Prince Eugene.'
'Why, 'twas a very wicked thing!'
   Said little Wilhelmine.
'Nay… nay… my little girl,' quoth he,
60 'It was a famous victory.

11

'And every body praised the Duke
   Who this great fight did win.'
'But what good came of it at last?'
   Quoth little Peterkin.
65 'Why that I cannot tell,' said he,
'But 'twas a famous victory.'

(1798)

The Soldier

Rupert Brooke (1887–1915)

IF I should die, think only this of me:
    That there's some corner of a foreign field
That is for ever England. There shall be
    In that rich earth a richer dust conceal'd;
5 A dust whom England bore, shaped, made aware,
    Gave, once, her flowers to love, her ways to roam,
A body of England's, breathing English air,
    Wash'd by the rivers, blest by suns of home.
And think, this heart, all evil shed away,
10   A pulse in the eternal mind, no less
      Gives somewhere back the thoughts by England given;
Her sights and sounds; dreams happy as her day;
    And laughter, learnt of friends; and gentleness,
      In hearts at peace, under an English heaven.

(1914; published 1915)

The Burial of Sir John Moore after Corunna

Charles Wolfe (1791–1823)

> General Sir John Moore (1761–1809) was mortally wounded in the battle of Corunna in 1809, part of the long war waged by Britain against Napoleon. The British lost the battle: *The Times* described it as 'a shameful disaster'.

Not a drum was heard, not a funeral note,
   As his corse to the rampart we hurried;
Not a soldier discharged his farewell shot
   O'er the grave where our hero we buried.

5 We buried him darkly at dead of night,
   The sods with our bayonets turning,
By the struggling moonbeam's misty light
   And the lanthorn dimly burning.

No useless coffin enclosed his breast,
10   Nor in sheet or in shroud we wound him;
But he lay like a warrior taking his rest
   With his martial cloak around him.

Few and short were the prayers we said,
   And we spoke not a word of sorrow;
15 But we steadfastly gazed on the face that was dead,
   And we bitterly thought of the morrow.

We thought, as we hollow'd his narrow bed
   And smooth'd down his lonely pillow,
That the foe and the stranger would tread o'er his head,
20   And we far away on the billow!

Lightly they'll talk of the spirit that's gone,
    And o'er his cold ashes upbraid him—
But little he'll reck, if they let him sleep on
    In the grave where a Briton has laid him.

25 But half of our heavy task was done
    When the clock struck the hour for retiring;
And we heard the distant and random gun
    That the foe was sullenly firing.

Slowly and sadly we laid him down,
30   From the field of his fame fresh and gory;
We carved not a line, and we raised not a stone,
    But left him alone with his glory.

                                (1817)

Incident of the French Camp
Robert Browning (1812–1889)

> Browning based his poem on a true story, though historically the hero was a man and not a boy. The battle of Ratisbon was fought between the Austrians and the French on 23 April 1809. Marshal Jean Lannes led the French troops into attack. The French Emperor, Napoleon I, watched the battle unfold.

1

You know, we French stormed Ratisbon:
   A mile or so away,
On a little mound, Napoleon
   Stood on our storming-day;
5 With neck out-thrust, you fancy how,
   Legs wide, arms locked behind,
As if to balance the prone brow
   Oppressive with its mind.

2

Just as perhaps he mused "My plans
10 "That soar, to earth may fall,
"Let once my army-leader Lannes
   Waver at yonder wall,"—
Out 'twixt the battery-smokes there flew
   A rider, bound on bound
15 Full-galloping; nor bridle drew
   Until he reached the mound.

3

Then off there flung in smiling joy,
   And held himself erect
By just his horse's mane, a boy:
   You hardly could suspect—
(So tight he kept his lips compressed,
   Scarce any blood came through)
You looked twice ere you saw his breast
   Was all but shot in two.

4

"Well," cried he, "Emperor, by God's grace
   "We've got you Ratisbon!
"The Marshal's in the market-place,
   "And you'll be there anon
"To see your flag-bird flap his vans
   "Where I, to heart's desire,
"Perched him!" The chief's eye flashed; his plans
   Soared up again like fire.

5

The chief's eye flashed; but presently
   Softened itself, as sheathes
A film the mother-eagle's eye
   When her bruised eaglet breathes;
"You're wounded!" "Nay," the soldier's pride
   Touched to the quick, he said:
"I'm killed, Sire!" And his chief beside
   Smiling the boy fell dead.

(1842)

From *Amours de Voyage*
Arthur Hugh Clough (1819–1861)

> This excerpt comes from a verse novel, set in the present day, which follows the adventures of Claude, an English tourist in Italy, at that time divided into many separate states. In February 1849 the people of Rome ousted their rulers and declared a republic, establishing a new 'National Guard'. Here Claude, a witness to the revolution, writes a letter home to his friend Eustace.

Claude to Eustace.

So, I have seen a man killed! An experience that, among others!
Yes, I suppose I have; although I can hardly be certain,
And in a court of justice could never declare I had seen it.
But a man was killed, I am told, in a place where I saw
5   Something; a man was killed, I am told, and I saw something.
I was returning home from St. Peter's[1]; Murray[2], as usual,
Under my arm, I remember; had crossed the St. Angelo bridge; and
Moving towards the Condotti[3], had got to the first
10   barricade, when
Gradually, thinking still of St. Peter's, I became conscious
Of a sensation of movement opposing me, — tendency this way
(Such as one fancies may be in a stream when the wave of
15   the tide is
Coming and not yet come, — a sort of poise and retention);
So I turned, and, before I turned, caught sight of stragglers
Heading a crowd, it is plain, that is coming behind that corner.

Looking up, I see windows filled with heads; the Piazza[4],
Into which you remember the Ponte St. Angelo enters,
Since I passed, has thickened with curious groups;
    and now the
Crowd is coming, has turned, has crossed that last
    barricade, is
Here at my side. In the middle they drag at something.
    What is it?
Ha! bare swords in the air, held up? There seem to be voices
Pleading and hands putting back; official, perhaps; but the
    swords are
Many, and bare in the air. In the air? they descend; they
    are smiting,
Hewing, chopping — At what? In the air once more
    upstretched? And —
Is it blood that's on them? Yes, certainly blood! Of
    whom, then?
Over whom is the cry of this furor[5] of exultation?
While they are skipping and screaming, and dancing their
    caps on the points of
Swords and bayonets, I to the outskirts back, and ask a
Mercantile-seeming bystander, 'What is it?' and he,
    looking always
That way, makes me answer, 'A Priest, who was trying to fly to
The Neapolitan army[6],' — and thus explains the proceeding.
You didn't see the dead man? No; — I began to be doubtful;
I was in black myself, and didn't know what
    mightn't happen,—

But a National Guard close by me, outside of the hubbub,
Broke his sword with slashing a broad hat covered with
    dust, — and
50 Passing away from the place with Murray under my arm, and
Stooping, I saw through the legs of the people the legs
    of a body.

(1849)

---

1 St Peter's St Peter's Basilica is the great church of Rome

2 Murray *Murray's Handbooks* were a famous series of guidebooks for British travellers

3 Condotti the Via Condotti is one of the most celebrated streets of Rome

4 Piazza … Ponte St Angelo the Ponte St Angelo ('the bridge of St Angelo') crosses the River Tiber and leads to a large square (or 'Piazza')

5 furor rage, madness, frenzy

6 Neapolitan army the army of another Italian state, Naples, a monarchy which sought to overturn the new republic

POWER, CONFLICT, AND VIOLENCE: INFLICTED HARMS

He fell among Thieves
Henry Newbolt (1862–1938)

> The poem is set in the remote Yasin valley in what is now Pakistan, which was at the time in which the poem is set the dangerous North-Western frontier of the British empire in India. The title alludes to a Biblical text (Luke, 10:30), at which point Jesus is beginning to tell the story of the Good Samaritan: 'And Jesus answering said, A certain man went down from Jerusalem to Jericho, and fell among thieves, which stripped him of his raiment, and wounded him, and departed, leaving him half dead.'

'Ye have robb'd,' said he, 'ye have slaughter'd and
   made an end,
     Take your ill-got plunder, and bury the dead:
What will ye more of your guest and sometime friend?'
5   'Blood for our blood,' they said.

He laugh'd: 'If one may settle the score for five,
     I am ready; but let the reckoning stand till day:
I have loved the sunlight as dearly as any alive.'
     'You shall die at dawn,' said they.

10 He flung his empty revolver down the slope,
     He climb'd alone to the Eastward edge of the trees;
All night long in a dream untroubled of hope
     He brooded, clasping his knees.

He did not hear the monotonous roar that fills
15   The ravine where the Yassîn river sullenly flows;
He did not see the starlight on the Laspur hills,
     Or the far Afghan snows.

He saw the April noon on his books aglow,
    The wisteria trailing in at the window wide;
He heard his father's voice from the terrace below
    Calling him down to ride.

He saw the gray little church across the park,
    The mounds that hid the loved and honour'd dead;
The Norman arch, the chancel softly dark,
    The brasses black and red.

He saw the School Close, sunny and green,
    The runner beside him, the stand by the parapet wall,
The distant tape, and the crowd roaring between,
    His own name over all.

He saw the dark wainscot and timber'd roof,
    The long tables, and the faces merry and keen;
The College Eight and their trainer dining aloof,
    The Dons on the daïs serene[1].

He watch'd the liner's stem ploughing the foam,
    He felt her trembling speed and the thrash of her screw;
He heard the passengers' voices talking of home,
    He saw the flag she flew.

And now it was dawn. He rose strong on his feet,
    And strode to his ruin'd camp below the wood;
He drank the breath of the morning cool and sweet:
    His murderers round him stood.

Light on the Laspur hills was broadening fast,
    The blood-red snow-peaks chill'd to a dazzling white;
He turn'd, and saw the golden circle at last,
    Cut by the Eastern height.

'O glorious Life, Who dwellest in earth and sun,
   I have lived, I praise and adore Thee.'
     A sword swept.
Over the pass the voices one by one
50   Faded, and the hill slept.

(1897)

---

1 **College Eight … serene** The protagonist of the poem is remembering his time as a student at Oxford or Cambridge University, eating in his college's dining hall. The 'College Eight' is a rowing crew. 'Dons' is a word for university teachers, who eat separately at 'high table', raised slightly on a platform (the 'daïs') above the rest of the tables in the dining hall.

An Irish Airman Foresees His Death
W.B. Yeats (1865–1939)

> The parish of Kiltartan is in County Galway, Ireland, and Kiltartan Cross is its principal crossroads. Yeats's great friend Lady Gregory lived nearby; and the subject of the poem is generally taken to be an imagined version of her son Robert, who joined the Royal Flying Corps and was killed in 1918.

I know that I shall meet my fate
Somewhere among the clouds above;
Those that I fight I do not hate,
Those that I guard I do not love;
5 My country is Kiltartan Cross,
My countrymen Kiltartan's poor,
No likely end could bring them loss
Or leave them happier than before.
Nor law, nor duty bade me fight,
10 Nor public men, nor cheering crowds,
A lonely impulse of delight
Drove to this tumult in the clouds;
I balanced all, brought all to mind,
The years to come seemed waste of breath,
15 A waste of breath the years behind
In balance with this life, this death.

(1918; published 1919)

POWER, CONFLICT, AND VIOLENCE: INFLICTED HARMS

The General
Siegfried Sassoon (1886–1967)

> One of the major offensives of World War I took place when the British launched an attack on the Germans from 9 April to 16 May 1917 near the French city of Arras. The fighting soon came to a stalemate, and by the battle's end there were nearly 160,000 British and 125,000 German casualties. Sassoon was a British officer.

'Good-morning; good-morning!' the General said
When we met him last week on our way to the line.
Now the soldiers he smiled at are most of 'em dead,
And we're cursing his staff for incompetent swine.
'He's a cheery old card,' grunted Harry to Jack
As they slogged up to Arras with rifle and pack.

. . . .

But he did for them both by his plan of attack.

(1917; published 1918)

Break of Day in the Trenches

Isaac Rosenberg (1890–1918)

The darkness crumbles away—
It is the same old druid[1] Time as ever.
Only a live thing leaps my hand—
A queer sardonic[2] rat—
5   As I pull the parapet's poppy
To stick behind my ear.
Droll rat, they would shoot you if they knew
Your cosmopolitan[3] sympathies.
Now you have touched this English hand
10 You will do the same to a German—
Soon, no doubt, if it be your pleasure
To cross the sleeping green between.
It seems you inwardly grin as you pass
Strong eyes, fine limbs, haughty athletes
15 Less chanced than you for life,
Bonds to the whims of murder,
Sprawled in the bowels of the earth,
The torn fields of France.
What do you see in our eyes
20 At the shrieking iron and flame
Hurled through still heavens?
What quaver—what heart aghast?
Poppies whose roots are in man's veins
Drop, and are ever dropping;
25 But mine in my ear is safe,
Just a little white with the dust.

(1916)

---

1 druid priest of an ancient, semi-legendary, pre-Christian religion
2 sardonic bitter, scornful, mocking
3 cosmopolitan belonging to all parts of the world; not confined to one nationality

In a Soldiers' Hospital I: Pluck
Eva Dobell (1876–1963)

> Eva Dobell volunteered to serve as a nurse during World War I.

Crippled for life at seventeen,
    His great eyes seem to question why:
With both legs smashed it might have been
    Better in that grim trench to die
5   Than drag maimed years out helplessly.

A child—so wasted and so white,
    He told a lie to get his way,
To march, a man with men, and fight
    While other boys are still at play.
10   A gallant lie your heart will say.

So broke with pain, he shrinks in dread
    To see the "dresser"[1] drawing near;
And winds the clothes about his head
    That none may see his heart-sick fear.
15   His shaking, strangled sobs you hear.

But when the dreaded moment's there
    He'll face us all, a soldier yet,
Watch his bared wounds with unmoved air,
    (Though tell-tale lashes still are wet),
20   And smoke his woodbine cigarette.

                (1916; published 1919)

---

[1] **dresser** a surgeon's assistant, whose job is to dress wounds

Disabled

Wilfred Owen (1893–1918)

He sat in a wheeled chair, waiting for dark,
And shivered in his ghastly suit of grey,
Legless, sewn short at elbow. Through the park
Voices of boys rang saddening like a hymn,
5   Voices of play and pleasure after day,
Till gathering sleep had mothered them from him.

About this time Town used to swing so gay
When glow-lamps budded in the light blue trees,
And girls glanced lovelier as the air grew dim,—
10   In the old times, before he threw away his knees.
Now he will never feel again how slim
Girls' waists are, or how warm their subtle hands;
All of them touch him like some queer disease.

There was an artist silly for his face,
15   For it was younger than his youth, last year.
Now, he is old; his back will never brace;
He's lost his colour very far from here,
Poured it down shell-holes till the veins ran dry,
And half his lifetime lapsed in the hot race,
20   And leap of purple spurted from his thigh.

One time he liked a blood-smear down his leg,
After the matches, carried shoulder-high.
It was after football, when he'd drunk a peg,
He thought he'd better join. —He wonders why.
25   Someone had said he'd look a god in kilts,
That's why; and may be, too, to please his Meg;
Aye, that was it, to please the giddy jilts

He asked to join. He didn't have to beg;
Smiling they wrote his lie; aged nineteen years.
30 Germans he scarcely thought of; all their guilt,
And Austria's, did not move him. And no fears
Of Fear came yet. He thought of jewelled hilts
For daggers in plaid socks; of smart salutes;
And care of arms; and leave; and pay arrears;
35 *Esprit de corps*; and hints for young recruits.
And soon, he was drafted out with drums and cheers.

Some cheered him home, but not as crowds cheer Goal.
Only a solemn man who brought him fruits
Thanked him; and then inquired about his soul.

40 Now, he will spend a few sick years in Institutes,
And do what things the rules consider wise,
And take whatever pity they may dole.
To-night he noticed how the women's eyes
Passed from him to the strong men that were whole.
45 How cold and late it is! Why don't they come
And put him into bed? Why don't they come?

(1917; published 1920)

Walking Wounded

Vernon Scannell (1922–2007)

    A mammoth morning moved grey flanks and groaned.
    In the rusty hedges pale rags of mist hung;
    The gruel of mud and leaves in the mauled lane
    Smelled sweet, like blood. Birds had died or flown,
5   Their green and silent attics sprouting now
    With branches of leafed steel, hiding round eyes
    And ripe grenades ready to drop and burst.
    In the ditch at the cross-roads the fallen rider lay
    Hugging his dead machine and did not stir
10 At crunch of mortar[1], tantrum of a Bren
    Answering a Spandau's[2] manic jabber.
    Then into sight the ambulances came,
    Stumbling and churning past the broken farm,
    The amputated sign-post and smashed trees,
15 Slow wagonloads of bandaged cries, square trucks
    That rolled on ominous wheels, vehicles
    Made mythopoeic by their mortal freight
    And crimson crosses on the dirty white.
    This grave procession passed, though, for a while,
20 The grinding of their engines could be heard,
    A dark noise on the pallor of the morning,
    Dark as dried blood; and then it faded, died.
    The road was empty, but it seemed to wait—
    Like a stage which knows the cast is in the wings—
25 Wait for a different traffic to appear.
    The mist still hung in snags from dripping thorns;
    Absent-minded guns still sighed and thumped.
    And then they came, the walking wounded,
    Straggling the road like convicts loosely chained,
30 Dragging at ankles exhaustion and despair.

Their heads were weighted down by last night's lead,
And eyes still drank the dark. They trailed the night
Along the morning road. Some limped on sticks;
Others wore rough dressings, splints and slings;
35 A few had turbanned heads, the dirty cloth
Brown-badged with blood. A humble brotherhood,
Not one was suffering from a lethal hurt,
They were not magnified by noble wounds,
There was no splendour in that company.
40 And yet, remembering after eighteen years,
In the heart's throat a sour sadness stirs;
Imagination pauses and returns
To see them walking still, but multiplied
In thousands now. And when heroic corpses
45 Turn slowly in their decorated sleep
And every ambulance has disappeared
The walking wounded still trudge down that lane,
And when recalled they must bear arms again.

(1965)

---

1 mortar explosive shells
2 Bren ... Spandau the Bren was the standard British gun, and the Spandau the German, during World War II

The Veteran

Mary Postgate Cole (1893–1980)

We came upon him sitting in the sun,
    Blinded by war, and left. And past the fence
There came young soldiers from the Hand and Flower,
    Asking advice of his experience.

5 And he said this, and that, and told them tales,
    And all the nightmares of each empty head
Blew into air; then, hearing us beside,
    "Poor chaps, how'd they know what it's like?" he said.

And we stood there, and watched him as he sat,
10   Turning his sockets where they went away,
Until it came to one of us to ask
"And you're—how old?"
    "Nineteen, the third of May."

(1918)

POWER, CONFLICT, AND VIOLENCE: INFLICTED HARMS

The Order

Michael Symmons Roberts (b. 1963)

She slid a chest beneath her childhood bed,
collecting for the day she set up home:
bequests, birthdays, every coin she spared

would go to buy a candle, cup, a spoon.
5 She kept them separate: silver, linen, plate,
curator of her future life's museum.

She married, mothered, held her household tight,
surrounded by the objects she had saved.
She kept the drawers and shelves immaculate.

10 Then one spring day they ordered her to leave.
She packed what she could carry in that chest.
The train was cramped; her children silent, brave.

And now her things are ordered like the rest:
a cloche[1] of knives and forks, a room of boots,
15 a plait of fading hair behind lit glass.

(2013)

---

1 cloche a transparent cover placed over tender plants by gardeners to protect them; here, by extension, a glass-covered display case

Gas Attack

Choman Hardi (b. 1974)

> This poem is from a sequence entitled 'Anfal', which draws on the testimony of survivors from the attacks mounted on rural Kurdistan by the Iraq government in 1988. Thousands of civilians were killed, many dying from the use of poison gas.

Badria Saeed Khidir and Ayshe Maghdid Mahmud

Bombs could fall anywhere, any time of the day.
They were a nuisance we got used to. In our
dug out shelters we felt safe, until that haunting

winter twilight when the muffled explosions
deceived us. We came out thinking we'd survived
the bombs but a chalky-yellow powder settled

on our skin, smelling of sweet apples at first,
seemed safe to breathe in. People were going crazy –
laughing, buckling at the knees, twisting, running

to the water source, blinded, bumping into trees.
Villagers from the region came to our aid. They said
my son looked strange, as if his eye-colour had spilt

out, his face was blistered, blackened. He groaned
like a calf faced with the knife. I was still blind when he
died, could not see him, did not say goodbye.

(2015)

The End of Summer

Roger McGough (b. 1937)

It is the end of summer
The end of day and cool,
As children, holiday-sated,
Idle happily home from school.

Dusk is slow to gather
The pavements still are bright,
It is the end of summer
And a bag of dynamite

Is pushed behind the counter
Of a department store, and soon
A trembling hand will put an end
To an English afternoon.

The sun on rooftops gleaming
Underlines the need to kill,
It is the end of summer
And all is cool, and still.

(1986)

The right word

Imitiaz Dharker (b. 1954)

Outside the door,
lurking in the shadows,
is a terrorist.

Is that the wrong description?
5   Outside that door,
taking shelter in the shadows,
is a freedom-fighter.

I haven't got this right.
Outside, waiting in the shadows,
10   is a hostile militant.

Are words no more
than waving, wavering flags?
Outside your door,
watchful in the shadows,
15   is a guerrilla warrior.

God help me.
Outside, defying every shadow,
stands a martyr.
I saw his face.

20   No words can help me now.
Just outside the door,
lost in shadows,
is a child who looks like mine.

One word for you.
25 Outside my door,
his hand too steady,
his eyes too hard
is a boy who looks like your son, too.

I open the door.
30 Come in, I say.
Come in and eat with us.

The child steps in
and carefully, at my door,
takes off his shoes.

(2006)

War Poetry
Kate Clanchy (b. 1965)

The class has dropped its books. The janitor's
disturbed some wasps, broomed the nest
straight off the roof. It lies outside, exotic
as a fallen planet, a burst city of the poor;
5   its newsprint halls, its ashen, tiny rooms
all open to the air. The insects' buzz
is low-key as a smart machine. They group,
regroup, in stacks and coils, advance
and cross like pulsing points on radar screens.

10   And though the boys have shaven heads
and football strips, and would, they swear,
enlist at once, given half a chance, yes,
march down Owen's[1] darkening lanes
to join the lads and stuff the Boche[2] –
15   they don't rush out to pike the nest,
or lap the yard with grapeshot faces.
They watch the wasps through glass,
silently, abashed, the way we all watch war.

(1995)

---

1 **Owen's** Wilfrid Owen (1893–1918), whose poem 'The Send-Off' begins picturing soldiers departing for the front: 'Down the close, darkening lanes they sang their way'
2 **Boche** a slang word for 'Germans', much used by British soldiers during World War I

From **To J.H. Reynolds, Esq.**

John Keats (1795–1821)

> This is an excerpt (lines 82–106) of a letter in verse that Keats wrote to a friend.

    It is a flaw
In happiness, to see beyond our bourn,–
It forces us in summer skies to mourn,
It spoils the singing of the Nightingale.

5   Dear Reynolds! I have a mysterious tale,
And cannot speak it: the first page I read
Upon a Lampit rock of green sea-weed
Among the breakers; 'twas a quiet eve,
The rocks were silent, the wide sea did weave
10 An untumultuous fringe of silver foam
Along the flat brown sand; I was at home
And should have been most happy, —but I saw
Too far into the sea, where every maw
The greater on the less feeds evermore.—
15 But I saw too distinct into the core
Of an eternal fierce destruction,
And so from happiness I far was gone.
Still am I sick of it, and tho', to-day,
I've gather'd young spring-leaves, and flowers gay
20 Of periwinkle and wild strawberry,
Still do I that most fierce destruction see, —
The Shark at savage prey,—the Hawk at pounce, —
The gentle Robin, like a Pard or Ounce,
Ravening a worm,—Away ye horrid moods!
25 Moods of one's mind!

                    (1818; published 1848)

Badger

John Clare (1793–1864)

    When midnight comes a host of dogs and men
    Go out and track the badger to his den,
    And put a sack within the hole, and lie
    Till the old grunting badger passes by.
5   He comes and hears — they let the strongest loose.
    The old fox hears the noise and drops the goose.
    The poacher shoots and hurries from the cry,
    And the old hare half wounded buzzes by.
    They get a forkèd stick to bear him down
10 And clap the dogs and take him to the town,
    And bait him all the day with many dogs,
    And laugh and shout and fright the scampering hogs.
    He runs along and bites at all he meets:
    They shout and hollo down the noisy streets.

15 He turns about to face the loud uproar
    And drives the rebels to their very door.
    The frequent stone is hurled where'er they go;
    When badgers fight, then every one's a foe.
    The dogs are clapt and urged to join the fray;
20 The badger turns and drives them all away.
    Though scarcely half as big, demure and small,
    He fights with dogs for hours and beats them all.
    The heavy mastiff, savage in the fray,
    Lies down and licks his feet and turns away.
25 The bulldog knows his match and waxes cold,
    The badger grins and never leaves his hold.
    He drives the crowd and follows at their heels
    And bites them through—the drunkard swears and reels.

The frighted women take the boys away,
30 The blackguard laughs and hurries on the fray.
He tries to reach the woods, an awkward race,
But sticks and cudgels quickly stop the chase.
He turns agen and drives the noisy crowd
And beats the many dogs in noises loud.
35 He drives away and beats them every one,
And then they loose them all and set them on.
He falls as dead and kicked by boys and men,
Then starts and grins and drives the crowd agen;
Till kicked and torn and beaten out he lies
40 And leaves his hold and cackles, groans, and dies.

                (between 1832 and 1837; published 1920)

Binsey Poplars

Gerard M. Hopkins (1844–1889)

felled 1879

My aspens dear, whose airy cages quelled,
Quelled or quenched in leaves the leaping sun,
All felled, felled, are all felled;
   Of a fresh and following folded rank
       Not spared, not one
         That dandled a sandalled
       Shadow that swam or sank
On meadow and river and wind-wandering weed-
   winding bank.

O if we but knew what we do
       When we delve or hew—
        Hack and rack the growing green!
         Since country is so tender
        To touch, her being só slender,
        That, like this sleek and seeing ball
        But a prick will make no eye at all,
        Where we, even where we mean
          To mend her we end her,
        When we hew or delve:
After-comers cannot guess the beauty been.
   Ten or twelve, only ten or twelve
       Strokes of havoc únselve
        The sweet especial scene,
       Rural scene, a rural scene,
       Sweet especial rural scene.

(1879; published 1918)

Acknowledgments

We are grateful for permission to include extracts from the following copyright material in this book:

Simon Armitage: 'Poem' from *Paper Aeroplane: Selected Poems* (Faber, 2001), copyright © Simon Armitage 2001, reprinted by permission of Faber & Faber Ltd.

Elizabeth Bishop: 'The Fish' from *The Complete Poems* (Chatto & Windus, 1969, 1983), reprinted by permission of The Random House Group Ltd.

Edmund Blunden: 'Forefathers' from *The Shepherd and Other Poems of Peace and War* (Cobden-Sanderson, 1922), reprinted by permission of David Higham Associates on behalf of the Estate of Edmund Blunden.

Charles Causley: 'Timothy Winters' from *Collected Poems: 1951-2000* (Picador, 2000), reprinted by permission of David Higham Associates on behalf of the Estate of Charles Causley.

Kate Clanchy: 'War Poetry' from *Selected Poems* (Picador, 2014), copyright © Kate Clanchy 2014, reprinted by permission of Pan Macmillan via PLSclear.

John Clare: 'Open Winter' from *John Clare, Poems of the Middle Period*, Vol 5, edited by Eric Robinson, David Pownall and P M S Dawson (OUP, Clarendon Press, 1996) and 'The Badger' from *The Later Poems of John Clare* edited by Eric Robinson, David Pownall and Margaret Grainger (OUP, Clarendon Press, 1984), reprinted by permission of Curtis Brown Group Ltd, London, on behalf of Eric Robinson.

Margaret Postgate Cole: 'The Veteran' from *Margaret Postgate's Poems* (Allen & Unwin, 1918), reprinted by permission of David Higham Associates on behalf of the Estate of Margaret Postgate Cole.

E E Cummings: 'anyone lived in a pretty how town', copyright © 1940, 1968, 1991 by the Trustees for the E E Cummings Trust, from *The Complete Poems 1904- 1962* edited by George J Firmage (Liveright, 1994), reprinted by permission of Liveright Publishing Corporation.

Imtiaz Dharker: 'the right word' from *The Terrorist at My Table* (Bloodaxe, 2006), copyright © Imtiaz Dharker 2006, reprinted by permission of Bloodaxe Books, www.bloodaxebooks.com.

Emily Dickinson: 'A narrow fellow in the grass' J 986/F 1096 from *The Poems of Emily Dickinson* edited by Thomas J Johnson (The Belknap Press, 1983), copyright © 1951, 1955, copyright © renewed 1979, 1983 by the President and Fellows of Harvard College; copyright © 1914, 1918, 1919, 1924, 1929, 1930, 1932, 1935, 1937, 1942 by Martha Dickinson Bianchi; copyright © 1952, 1957, 1958, 1963, 1965 by Mary L Hampson; reprinted by permission of Harvard University Press.

Carol Ann Duffy: 'A Child's Sleep' from *Meeting Midnight* (Faber, 1999), copyright © Carol Ann Duffy 1995, reprinted by permission of the author c/o Rogers, Coleridge & White Ltd, 20 Powis Mews, London W11 1JN.

T S Eliot: 'Virginia' from *Collected Poems 1909-1962* (Faber, 1963), reprinted by permission of Faber & Faber Ltd.

James Fenton: 'Hinterhof' from *Yellow Tulips 1968-2011* (Faber, 2012) from *New Selected Poems* (Penguin 2006), reprinted by permission of Faber & Faber Ltd.

Leontia Flynn: 'My Father's Language' from *Profit and Loss* (Cape, 2011), reprinted by permission of The Random House Group Ltd.

Robert Frost: 'Putting in the Seed' from *The Poetry of Robert Frost* edited by Edward Connery Lathem (Jonathan Cape, 1971), reprinted by permission of The Random House Group Ltd.

Sophie Hannah: 'Squirrel's the Word', copyright © Sophie Hannah 2003, from *Marrying the Ugly Millionaire: New and Collected Poems* (Carcanet, 2015), reprinted by permission of Carcanet Press Ltd.

Choman Hardi: 'Gas Attack' from *Considering the Women* (Bloodaxe, 2016), copyright © Choman Hardi 2066, reprinted by permission of Bloodaxe Books, www.bloodaxebooks.com

Tony Harrison: 'Clearing 1' from *Collected Poems* (Viking, 2007), reprinted by permission of Faber & Faber Ltd.

Seamus Heaney: 'Digging' from *Death of a Naturalist* (Faber, 1968), copyright © Seamus Heaney 1968, reprinted by permission of Faber & Faber Ltd.

Tracey Herd: 'You Can't Take My World With You' from *Not in This World* (Bloodaxe, 2015), copyright © Tracey Herd 2015, reprinted by permission of Bloodaxe Books, www.bloodaxebooks.com

Ted Hughes: 'The Jaguar' from *The Hawk in the Rain* (Faber, 1957), copyright © Ted Hughes 1957, and 'Full Moon and Little Frieda' from *Wodwo* (Faber, 1967), copyright © Ted Hughes 1967, reprinted by permission of Faber & Faber Ltd.

Kathleen Jamie: 'The White-Sided Dolphins' from *The Tree House* (Picador, 2004), copyright © Kathleen Jamie 2004, reprinted by permission of Pan Macmillan via PLSclear.

Philip Larkin: 'The Trees' and 'First Sight' from *Collected Poems* edited by Anthony Thwaite (Faber, 2003), reprinted by permission of Faber & Faber Ltd.

Norman MacCaig: 'Aunt Julia' from *The Poems of Norman MacCaig* edited by Ewen MacCaig (Polygon, 2005), copyright © Norman MacCaig, reprinted by permission of the publisher Birlinn Ltd via PLSclear.

Roger McGough: 'Bad Day at the Ark' from The Way Things Are (Viking, 1999), and 'The End of Summer' from *Melting Into the Foreground* (Viking, 1986), reprinted by permission of Peters Fraser & Dunlop (www.petersfraserdunlop.com) on behalf of Roger McGough.

Grace Nichols: 'Praise Song for My Mother' from *The Fat Black Woman's Poems* (Virago, 1984), copyright © Grace Nichols 1984, reprinted by permission of Little, Brown Book Group Ltd.

Bernard O'Donoghue: 'The Robin in Autumn' from *Gunpowder* (Chatto, 1995), copyright © Bernard O'Donoghue 1995, reprinted by permission of the author.

Michael Symmons Roberts: 'The Order' from *Drysalter* (Cape, 2013), reprinted by permission of The Random House Group Ltd.

Siegfried Sassoon: 'The General' from *Collected Poems 1908-1956* (Faber, 1956), copyright © Siegfried Sassoon, reprinted by permission of the Estate of George Sassoon c/o Barbara Levy Literary Agency.

Vernon Scannell: 'Walking Wounded' from *New and Collected Poems 1950-1993* (Faber, 2013), reprinted by permission of the Estate of Vernon Scannell.

E J Scovell: 'Growing Girl' from *Collected Poems* (Carcanet, 1988), reprinted by permission of Carcanet Press Ltd.

Jo Shapcott: 'Cabbage Dreams', copyright © Jo Shapcott 1998, from *Her Book: Poems 1988-1998* (Faber 2000), first published in *My Life Asleep* (OUP, 1998), reprinted by permission of Faber & Faber Ltd.

Jon Silkin: 'Death of a Son (who died in a mental hospital aged one)' from *Selected Poems* (Sinclair Stevenson, 1993), reprinted by permission of The Random House Group Ltd.

Stephen Spender: 'My Parents' from *Collected Poems 1928-1953* (Faber, 1955), copyright © Stephen Spender 1995, reprinted by permission of the Estate of Stephen Spender c/o Ed Victor Ltd.

Anne Stevenson: 'Poem for a Daughter' from *Poems 1955-2005* (Bloodaxe 2005), copyright © Anne Stevenson 2005, reprinted by permission of Bloodaxe Books, www.bloodaxebooks.com

Arundhathi Subramaniam: 'I Speak for Those with Orange Lunch Boxes' from *When God is a Traveller* (Bloodaxe, 2014), copyright © Arundhathi Subramaniam 2014, reprinted by permission of Bloodaxe Books, www.bloodaxebooks.com

Kate Tempest: 'For My Niece' from *Hold Your Own* (Picador, 2014), copyright © Kate Tempest 2004, reprinted by permission of the author, c/o Johnson & Alcock.

Hugo Williams: 'Mirror, Windows' from *Collected Poems* (Faber, 2002), reprinted by permission of Faber & Faber Ltd.

The publisher and authors would also like to thank the following for permission to use photographs and other copyright material:

Cover: © Ron Jones/Trevillion Images. All other images © Shutterstock.

We have tried to trace and contact all copyright holders before publication. If notified, the publishers will be pleased to rectify any errors or omissions at the earliest opportunity.

Any third party use of this material outside of this publication is prohibited. Interested parties should apply to the copyright holders indicated in each case.